Six Years Lost

Benjamin J. Schmidt
with Brian Scott

9FOOT
VOICE

www.9footvoice.com

9 Foot Voice - Minnesota

Cover design by Erin Nausin
www.theprimaverastudio.com

ISBN: 978-0-9968432-4-9

To my Aunt Judy, Cousin Tony and Grampa Jim.
We miss you.

Contents

Forward

As an inner city surgeon, I know the world Ben describes in this book. I see the direct results of the violence and I spend my days patching it up. So first, we need to celebrate what Ben is doing. He's standing up and talking openly about what happened. He's shining light into a dark world. This is risky, and it takes the kind of guts most people don't have.

First, let's celebrate, but then we have to get to work. This book has something to teach us, and we need to pay close attention because Ben is a subtle teacher. He doesn't come right out and tell you, but if you open your eyes to watch for it, you will see Jesus on every page.

Watch how many times Ben was protected, how many times God was holding his hand, how many times there was a path unraveling to move him towards healing. God kept showing up, orchestrating opportunities for Ben to slow his destruction and turn his life around.

And Ben was desperate for healing. He wasn't always

aware of it, but he had a thirst only Jesus could quench. If you watch for it, you'll see that thirst on every page of the book as well.

Ben's thirst was physical as well as spiritual. I see it in patients on meth all the time. They come into our trauma center and won't move for three days. When they wake up they pound down the water. They won't say a word at first; they'll look me in my eyes, drink two cups as fast as they can then ask for another.

Ben talks about this thirst. And he talks about how he thirsted for respect, for attention, for power, for money and drugs - he gulped down all of these things until he finally learned they wouldn't help. They couldn't quench anything. They only made him more thirsty.

But God never gave up on Ben. Watch for it as you read this book. This is a story of redemption. It's a story of a man healed. It's a story of Jesus showing up every day with a bucket of cold water offering again and again until we listen, "Here I am! I am the living water. Come quench your thirst."

- Tom Blee, MD
Creator and Co-Director of LIFEteam,
a hospital-based intervention program
Author of <u>How to Save a Surgeon</u>

Introduction

My childhood was fairly typical, which, in a way, makes my story more disturbing. I grew up outside of Diamond Bluff, Wisconsin, in a comfortable home along the Mississippi river. My mom was a real estate agent and my dad had a good job at the power plant. Their divorce when I was eight was difficult, of course, but not devastating. My step-father was an elementary school principal and a good man.

It would be easier if I had some circumstance or some other person to blame for my choices. It is tempting, for example, to point a finger at my brother, Jesse. He was three years older and hung out with a rough crowd from an early age. But as much as I'd like to shift some of my guilt, it wouldn't be honest. My younger sister had both Jesse and me, two older brothers heavily involved in crime and drugs, but she was able to keep clean of it all.

No, I made my own decisions. I chose my path.

This book tells the story of that path. It begins when

- at nine years old - I made my first conscious choice to cross into the darkness, and it ends at twenty-two when the grace of God dragged me back into the light. It is a grim story - in my early twenties I didn't believe I'd live long enough to see a new year much less get healthy - and one I never imagined I would tell. For a long time I looked back at the six years I lost to drugs with nothing but shame. I never spoke of it. I tried not to think about it.

Then I started working out at a new gym. There, I met Dr. Tom Blee, a trauma surgeon who worked in Saint Paul. He worked with gang kids and had witnessed the effects of drugs first hand on the lives of young men and women. And he was on fire for Jesus, trying to bring healing into the vicious circle of despair and violence he encountered every day.

Tom introduced me to a man named John Turnipseed. Mr. Turnipseed was a former dealer and pimp, and his family used to rule the gang scene in Minneapolis. But Jesus had turned his life around until he had become a pastor and community leader in the same neighborhood he had previously based his criminal operations.

Tom and John inspired me to see my story in a different light. I knew I had some extraordinary experiences. Even before I was 21 I had thought I should write some of them down. But for the first time I understood my story could be useful. Through these men, I saw how God used dark memories of the past for healing in the present.

Tom then introduced me to Brian Scott, a former

pastor who now helped people write their stories. His background was perfect in helping create a book about escaping hell on earth.

A few weeks later we sat down at a local restaurant and I began to share my journey. At first it hurt. I'd tell a story then realize one person was in prison, and two others had died. It shocked me how many people from that life were no longer with us. There are no happy endings in that world, except for those who are able to escape.

It was also difficult to revisit the traumas. My life has been profoundly affected by suicide, and remembering those I had lost reopened old wounds. The grief compounded as - in the last few months of preparing this book for release - two more dear friends took their own lives.

As hard as it was, some things became more and more clear as I told my story. First, there are no coincidences; everything happens for a reason. And second, life has meaning; God has a purpose for us all.

Because of this, I believe I have a story worth telling. It is a story, after all, about the love of God rescuing someone from the very belly of the beast. And I pray that it helps others, maybe even you, to know that even in the darkest shadow, there is always hope. Your life has worth. Even when you think you are totally alone, God is there. With Jesus there is no such thing as too far gone, too broken, or too messed up. He is at work in your life right now though you may not know it. No matter how bad you might think you are, you too can be healed.

Note: The stories in this book are true, and I did my best to tell them honestly. However, it is not my intent to expose others who were - or still are - part of that world. Their stories, and their paths to healing are their own, and are not mine to tell.

To that end, in order to protect the identities of those involved, we have changed names and identifying details, and adjusted some timelines.

1995-2003

The Lord is my shepherd; I shall not want. He makes me to lie down in green pastures; He leads me beside the still waters. He restores my soul; He leads me in the paths of righteousness for His name's sake. Yea, though I walk through the valley of the shadow of death, I will fear no evil; For You are with me; Your rod and Your staff, they comfort me. You prepare a table before me in the presence of my enemies; You anoint my head with oil; My cup runs over. Surely goodness and mercy shall follow me all the days of my life; And I will dwell in the house of the Lord. Forever. The Lord is my shepherd; I shall not want. He makes me to lie down in green pastures; He leads me beside the still waters. He restores my soul; He leads me in the paths of righteousness for His name's sake. Yea, though I walk through the valley of the shadow of death, I will fear no evil; For You are with me; Your rod and Your staff, they comfort me. You prepare a table before me in the presence of my enemies; You anoint my head with oil; My cup runs over. Surely

Matchbook

I sprinted along the gravel shoulder with my skateboard tucked under an arm. At the top of the hill I slowed to a trot, then a walk, then I stopped. The highway stretched along the river for a half mile before turning out of sight. I had been following my brother Jesse and his friend Derek since they left the house. They hadn't seen me, I was sure of it, and there was no place for them to go. I pulled hard at my ear, squinting at the empty road, but they had disappeared.

I coasted down the hill on my skateboard, crouching low. The wheels vibrated on the pavement and my stomach buzzed into my throat until the road flattened, slowing me to a stop. The scent of the river mixed with the smell of hot asphalt. Wind blew through the corn field on my left, otherwise it was quiet.

They were gone and it was time to give up the game. I turned back towards our house but before I made it more than a few steps I heard my brother's laugh. I snapped my head, searching for the source, and stared down a driveway on the far side of the highway. It twisted back to a trailer home.

A hole bloomed in my gut, shuddered to my knees and made me queasy. I knew the house and hated it. A man with greasy hair could often be seen mowing the front yard. His face would lift to our car as we passed, his eyes shadowed in darkness. I was nine-years old and knew as children do that he was a monster.

There was no sign of the man, but I gripped my skateboard against my chest like a shield. I faced a terrible choice. I could never imagine myself walking down that driveway alone, but I couldn't bear to go home, not without seeing what my brother was doing.

From the other side of the house, I heard metal scraping against metal. My brother and his friend were doing something exciting, I could feel it. I gulped down air, trying to catch my breath, and before I could think it through, I hurried across the road.

Trees snarled close on both sides of the driveway. The day, warm a second ago, grew chilly. After a dozen steps, I imagined a murderer behind me and broke into a sprint, not stopping until I skidded into the backyard.

"What the hell?" My brother's friend Derek was thirteen years old, but as tall as my dad. He wore black jeans and a shirt with letters scrawled in jagged lines like they were bleeding. A cluster of angry red zits covered his forehead. He had been kicking at a bent metal pole - one half of a broken clothes line - but stopped to scowl at me. "What are you doing back here?"

I couldn't catch my breath to answer.

"You following us?"

I scanned the backyard for my brother Jesse. There were weeds sprouting around the foundation, a broken lawn chair, a rusted out grill, but no sign of him.

"Hey little shit, I'm talking to you."

A thin curl of fear tightened around my spine; I took a careful step back.

"Get the fuck out of here," Derek said.

A breeze picked up and I caught the smell of an animal rotting in the woods.

"Get out!" he said.

Derek picked up a rock the size of his fist. I turned my shoulder from him, but wanted to keep him in my line of vision. I clenched up, ready for the blow, but a creak from the front door distracted him.

"Hey dumbass, where did you come from?" My brother stepped onto the landing and I almost shouted with relief. Like Derek, he was thirteen, but skinnier with dark shaggy hair. He stood cocky, slanting against the railing. I studied every movement, his tone of voice, hoping to imitate it later. "Come on in," he said and laughed strangely, giving a look to Derek I didn't understand.

Derek whooped and dropped the rock. Forgetting about me, he leapt up the few steps onto the landing and followed my brother inside. I stared after him.

Behind the door was nothing but shadow. My eyes darted to my skateboard which I had leaned against a tree. Either a terrible old man lurked in the darkness or I'd be breaking into someone's house. No matter what,

I should head home.

"You coming, dumbass?" Jesse grinned from the doorway and my doubts drizzled away.

It wasn't a hard sell. I knew it was wrong, but I had done bad things before. Just a few nights earlier I had spent the night at my cousin Tony's house. When my aunt sent us to bed we laid on the floor of his room, whispering furiously until finally she turned off the hall light and went to bed.

A few minutes later we had snuck out the back door. We crept three houses down and squatted in a drive-way. As lights from a TV flickered against the drapes, Tony pulled out the stink bomb we had bought at the Goodhue County Fair. It had an aluminum wrapper, like a candy bar. When we yanked away the seal it puffed full of air. Quickly, Tony taped it to the man's front door. We counted to thirty and rang the doorbell.

We scurried off - neither of us had thought to hide and watch - sprinting through back yards to Tony's house. After sneaking back through the sliding door, we collapsed in a heap in his room.

The idea of the man opening the door to nothing but the stink of rotten eggs made me laugh so hard I couldn't breathe. Tony rolled, howling on the floor. Eventually his mom pounded on the door, telling us to quiet down.

I told myself that sneaking into a strange man's trailer home was the same as planting a stink bomb. The parts that felt different, more serious, dangerous, I shoved aside. It was time to act; I had already done too much thinking and if I hesitated any longer Jesse would think I was scared. I took a breath, jogged up to the porch and stepped in.

I immediately regretted it. The old man, thank goodness, wasn't there, but the smell of cat piss and cigarettes almost pushed me over. Smudges on the windows blocked most of the light.

Jesse had stepped back to the kitchen and started rummaging through the fridge. Derek stood between us. He had a drinking glass in his hand; gave it a little toss and caught it. Then he shouted, "Catch!" and whipped it in my direction. I flinched as the glass shattered on the floor between us. He laughed - almost a bark - as I stared at the mess.

My weak excuses started falling apart. This was all wrong and I knew it. My mom raised me right. Sure, she and my dad divorced the year before and it had been difficult, but I was still a good kid from a stable home. Just that morning, my mom had taken me to church. My knees pressed against the pad as I had reached out for the wafer. Shoot, my shirt could still smell like incense. And now, a couple hours later, I knew what I was doing was a sin.

"Look at him," Jesse said. He and Derek stared at me. "Loosen up, Dude."

I tried. I leaned against the wall, slanting my body like my brother had, and forced a smile.

My brother laughed. "Listen, dumbass. Guy's not here. If we hear his car we'll take off."

I wanted to take off immediately, but I nodded.

My brother snorted. "I'm checking the basement," he said and disappeared behind a door off the kitchen.

Derek said, "Right behind you," but didn't move. In-stead, he snatched a box of matches off the table. He lit one and dropped it. The flame wisped into smoke before it hit the linoleum. He pushed his shoe into the ember.

He glared up at me. "What is your problem, ya little shit?"

I didn't dare look away. Derek lit another match and tossed it at me. It spun into smoke.

"Stop staring at me." He lit another match. "Fuckin' goon eyes." He tossed it.

My heart thumped painfully in my chest, but I knew not to provoke him. He had me cornered and it was best to draw into myself, to become as quiet and small as I could, until he lost interest. I slowed my breathing and backed into the wall.

He stepped close, threw a lit match. "You gotta light-en up, Benny." He tossed another; the red ember landed on my bare knee, giving a sharp poke of pain. I squat-ted down to brush it off, but kept quiet.

He threw another one; it landed on my shoe. I peeked up - his face was blank. Two feet away now, he lit an-other a match.

"Hey," my brother said. "You gotta come check this out."

Derek dropped the match and turned away. "I'm coming," he said. Done with me, he followed my broth-er downstairs.

I breathed as the two disappeared and leaned back against the wall. I could feel my heart beat behind my eyes, but tried not to freak out. Tried to shake it off.

"Hey dumbass, get down here."

I followed mechanically. The basement was a single room thick with dust. An old sofa sat under a window - the window had been broken by my brother to get in. Beer bottles and rolling papers covered a coffee table. A shelf containing hundreds of cassette tapes travelled the entire length of the wall.

Jesse rifled through them, dropping most on the ground but shoving a couple into the pocket of his jeans.

"Here." He shoved a tape at me.

It had Billy Ray Cyrus on the cover. I looked up at Jesse; he was grinning. Derek muttered in the corner but he seemed to drift far away; the matches, the stink, the sin fading with him. My brother had given me a gift. I felt like I had passed some test. He wanted me there and I could be part of his crew.

We left soon after. The tape scratched against my thigh as I kicked my skateboard down the road. On bikes, Derek and Jesse quickly pulled away from me, but I didn't mind. I'd follow my big brother anywhere - no matter how dark things would get.

"What do you think? If a man owns a hundred
sheep, and one of them wanders away, will he not leave
the ninety-nine on the hills and go to look for the one
that wandered off? And if he finds it, truly I tell you, he
is happier about that one sheep than about the ninety-nine that did not wander off. In the same way your
Father in heaven is not willing that any of these little
ones should perish.   -Matthew 18:12-14

Ecstasy

I laid on the couch with the phone to my ear and sunlight draining from the room as Alyssa talked. We were both sixteen and next to my cousin, Tony, she was my closest friend. In quiet voices, we talked about everything: frustrations with our parents, hopes for the future… and her boyfriend. Though she had been my first crush, the door had closed on us dating.

When I hung up, the house felt empty and so quiet I could hear the clock ticking on the wall. Light tumbled in from the kitchen. I stood, stretched, and moved to the oven, seconds before my frozen pizza was done.

A minute later, headlights streaked across the wall, then the thud of slamming car doors came muffled through the window. I finished slicing my pizza as Jesse stepped through the front door, his girlfriend trailing behind. He looked hollow, his eyes sunken into his face. He was nineteen; he had moved out the year before and was living in a house with a man who would soon go to prison for murder.

He snagged a piece of pizza. "Where's Mom?"

"Work."

"Yeah?" He took a bite and cursed at me when it burned the roof of his mouth. He grabbed my coke off the table.

"Hey!"

"Relax, man. Here," he dug a bottle of Advil from his pocket. "I brought you something." He knocked a few pills onto his palm, pinched one and dropped it on the table in front of me.

I peered at it, but kept my distance. It was round, smaller than an Advil, and had a professional-looking stamp on it. Whatever it was, it looked well made.

He gave me a hazy smile. "It's ecstasy, dumbass."

I blinked from the pill to my brother. I had no idea what the little pill would do and was half convinced it would kill me. "Thanks," I said.

He watched me expectantly. I needed to buy some time so I pointed down the hall and said, "Give me a second."

I raided my mom's liquor closet for vodka and mixed it in orange juice. When I came back to the table, Jesse and his girlfriend had moved into the living room, but the pill was still there. I took a long pull from my drink then wiped my mouth with my sleeve. I could lie to Jesse easily. I could throw the pill away or shove it in my pocket. But though seven years had passed I was still the same kid who'd do anything to impress his big brother. I took a sip of my drink then, quickly so as not to lose my nerve, I popped the pill to the back of my throat and swallowed hard.

I took a few breaths, checking for immediate effects. Nothing. In the living room, my brother and his girlfriend sprawled on the couch. I joined them with a goofy grin, weirdly proud of myself, but they ignored me.

I wasn't sure what I was supposed to do next. They were in the way of the television so I couldn't play Xbox and I didn't want to hang in my room. With a shrug, I squeezed behind the computer desk in the corner, turned on some music and played DJ. After about twenty minutes I queued up a track by Sisqo - The Thong Song. I had put it on as kind of a joke, honestly, but halfway through the screen began to melt and hug my eyes.

It was weird. I had smoked pot with my brother but never cared for it. Pot slowed me down and made me feel out of control. This, on the other hand, was otherworldly. The chorus, *Thong thong thong thong thong* became poetry. I ran my finger along the plastic edge of the computer and a warm fuzz spread up to my elbow. The music vibrated through me and I almost wept with affection for my brother, my mom, the sofa, the piece of lint I found on my pant leg. Everything glowed.

I floated into the kitchen for a glass of water. I gulped it down, and cold spread through my chest, making me hum. When I returned to the living room, my brother's girlfriend was slouching on the couch.

"Where's Jesse?"

She shrugged and I loved her for it.

With a series of thumps and a flurry of movement, Jesse rolled sideways down the stairs like he was in an action movie. He hit the bottom giggling, a dull black smudge gripped in his hand. I didn't have time to react before he raised a pistol towards my face and pulled the trigger.

Two sharp pains hit my neck and chest and for one dark moment I thought I was dead.

I touched my neck expecting it to be smeared with blood, but my fingers found nothing but skin. My brother sat in the corner laughing his ass off. He had shot me with an AirSoft gun, a toy which fired plastic BBs. He was such an ass and it was so stupid I started laughing with him.

The rest of the night we spent messing around, shooting these guns at each other. When we got sick of that game, we slid back and forth on the kitchen floor in our socks. Looking back, it was one of the last times I felt like a kid.

Hours later, the guns had been forgotten, the music turned down low and Jesse and I slumped on the couch; his girlfriend had curled up in the chair. I was still more than a little high.

Jesse leaned in, grinning. "You like this shit?"

"Yeah," I said. "I like it."

"You want to buy some?"

"I don't know. Maybe."

"Sell some to your friends?"

I shrugged.

"Listen, man, it's easy money." He talked to me seriously, explaining how the pricing worked. He told me

I could make a lot of cash and quickly. I didn't see the hungry look in his eyes, the way his cheeks had caved in; he was nineteen, living on his own, into cool shit. I admired him and he was treating me as an equal.

"Sounds great," I said.

"You got cash?"

I did - from my part-time job washing dishes - up in my room. I brought down a wad of twenties and counted them out on the table.

"That's all I have."

"No problem." He grinned at me. "I'll front you."

I shrugged. I didn't know what it meant but I wasn't going to ask.

"Just means you can pay me back later, dumbass."

Out of the white Advil bottle he carefully counted pills onto the coffee table. The lights were dim, party music was playing over the computer speakers, there was a cute girl sleeping on the easy chair, and the whole thing seemed badass - to have a pile of pills splayed out next to a stack of cash. We were drug dealers in an action movie; that we were the villains only made it sweeter.

The next day I called a friend and offered him $30 per pill or $50 for two. He had $50 but didn't have a car. As I only paid $3 a piece for them, it was a small problem; it only meant I would have to deliver. He lived about twenty miles away.

Before I left, I knocked a pill into my palm and swallowed it down with a coke. Then I called my brother.

"What do you want?"

"I made my first sale."

"Yeah?" His voice was flat.

"I got to deliver, but yeah."

"Cool."

"And I just took a hit myself," I said. "A few minutes ago."

He laughed and his voice brightened. "Check if Mom's got any Vick's Vapor rub in the bathroom."

The drug started kicking in and I got distracted by the feeling of the phone against my ear.

"If she does," Jesse said, "spread some of that shit on your face and stick your head out the window."

"Why?"

"Because it feels good, dumbass." With that he hung up.

Curious - and again I was high - I found Vapor Rub under the bathroom sink and rubbed it over my face and neck. As soon as I hit the highway I hung my face out the window and giggled into the wind. Jess was right; it did feel good. But then I was a stupid kid with bleach blond hair driving down the highway with my head hanging out the window like a dog. It was ten o'clock at night. I was on ecstasy. I was hustling a product.

Everything felt good.

For now we see only a reflection as in a mirror; then we shall see face to face. Now I know in part; then I shall know fully, even as I am fully known.
                                          - 1 Corinthians 13:12

The Ocean

Tires crunched in the gravel outside. I peered out the window and saw Tony's car. He had pulled into our driveway but stopped only a few yards in. My phone rang. The conversation which followed I've since replayed a thousand times in my head.

I said, "Hey Tony, what's up?"

"Not much." He sounded tired. We were seventeen and had grown out of stink bombs but he was still my best friend. His mom, my aunt Judy, was a second mother. I spent almost as many nights at his place as my own. We had spent countless hours over the years exploring his neighborhood, climbing trees and playing video games.

"You okay?"

He said, "Yeah, but I'm not up to hanging out tonight."

"No problem," I said. We didn't have much planned

beyond watching TV. I assumed he had a cold and didn't think much of it. "Hope you feel better."

He hung up, backed his car out of my driveway and drove away.

I grabbed a snack and turned on the television. I sunk into the couch with my feet up while - ten miles away - Tony walked alone into a dark house.

Two hours later my phone rang; it was my friend Travis. He was interrupting the fourth season finale of The Sopranos and I almost let him go to voicemail, but it was strange for him to call me so late, so I answered.

He barely had to speak before I knew something had happened. I assumed in those first moments it would be something manageable. Something we would all get through in time. But then Travis said my cousin's name, and my world fell apart.

I couldn't quite breathe right. My stomach and chest seized up. I was sitting, which was good. Travis talked and I tried to listen but his voice grew distant - not softer, but farther away.

Thirty minutes earlier, Travis had driven by my cousin's house and saw the light on in his bedroom so he decided to stop. He knocked on the front door, but no one answered. He knocked again and harder, but nothing. Music came thudding from my cousin's bedroom, so he stepped across the lawn a few feet, with the idea of tapping on his window which faced the street. He pushed through a bush and came up next to the glass. For a moment, he thought my cousin had started to repaint his walls. But that moment passed all too quickly as the horror of the situation became clear.

Tony had shot himself.

By the time Travis finished telling this story I had shut down into a terrible numbness. I heard myself ask, "Did you call 911?" and still remember his silence on the other side of the phone. I stared at the wall as Tony Soprano talked nonsense on the television. We probably said some other words but I don't remember. My fingers were trembling and I couldn't press the button when I tried to hang up the phone.

Everything from that point became hazy. I remember staring at the dark ceiling as I laid in bed. I remember my mom forcing me to eat some eggs. I remember sitting in my car with the engine off until my fingers went numb.

I remember walking the ashes of my cousin and best friend down the aisle of Saint Paul's Lutheran Church.

Weeks passed. The world darkened and turned cold. I didn't sleep at night then struggled to get out of bed in the morning. Everything felt wrong and I was blank inside. Still, I somehow kept moving forward. I showed up for school. I went to work. I convinced everyone I was okay.

My aunt Judy, however, didn't convince anyone. Tony was her only child; the only thing she had. She should have moved out of that house immediately, and we should have insisted on it, but memories of Tony kept her there. We hired a professional cleaner to fix his bedroom and she somehow continued on. Every day, more or less, she drove up to the Twin Cities to work a shift as a nurse for a children's hospital. Every day she came home alone to that house.

She spiraled deeper into herself and the family grew more and more worried. I was a mess myself, but I moved into her spare bedroom for awhile. Like I said, she had always been a second mother to me, and we thought my presence might help. I thought it might help me too - give me something productive to do.

I tried to be around in the evenings. She didn't talk much and when she did her thoughts seemed far away. But I think she appreciated having another person in the house; moving around, watching TV, warming food in the microwave.

Most days I drove directly to work after school, but one afternoon I needed to pick something up at Judy's house. Her car was in the driveway, but when I stepped through the front door the house felt empty. "Judy?" I called.

There was no response.

My body felt heavy as I walked into the living room. I stopped to breathe and I heard children's music coming from my cousin's room. I recognized it from a goofy CD we would play when we were little kids.

I put my hand against the wall to steady myself. I struggled to get enough air in my lungs to speak. "Judy?" I said again. The door to Tony's room was closed. I reached for the handle but didn't have the strength to turn it. A moment went on forever before I heard a quiet thump then the creak of a bed frame. When the door opened it felt like a miracle.

"Are you okay?"

Judy was wearing one of his shirts. She didn't look at me. "I'm okay," she said.

"Do you need anything?"

"No," she said.

I nodded and turned back towards the living room.

"Hey Ben?"

A new song came on the CD player: a man singing about zoo animals.

"Could you…" her voice was dreamy. "Do you know how to unload a gun?" She pointed into my cousin's room. A pistol sunk into the covers of the bed. Sick to my stomach, I grabbed it and removed the bullets. Then I hurried outside, shoved it in the trunk of my car, and called my mom.

Twenty minutes later the two of us went through the house, removing anything a person might use to hurt themselves. We left a couple kitchen knives because my aunt liked to cook, but otherwise cleaned it out.

After that, we tried to keep an eye on her. My mom checked in every day. I spent as much time as I could at the house. But no matter what we did, she continued to spiral. She wandered through the house at odd hours. She barely ate. She rarely spoke and when she did it was without emotion.

My mom grew desperate. Sadly, Tony wasn't her first experience with suicide: her dad had taken his own life while she was pregnant with me. Terrified she would lose her sister too, a few weeks after the incident with the gun she told Judy we were going on a road trip. In first grade my aunt brought me and Tony to Florida, so in honor of that we packed up the car and aimed for Cocoa Beach.

My aunt spent the drive staring blankly at the blur

of small towns and corn fields out the window. When we stopped for food she'd fuss with her french fries and complain her stomach hurt.

Two days later we pulled into the parking lot of a cheap motel off the interstate. My aunt went to bed early and stayed in her room until late in the morning. After lunch - I don't think she ate anything - we drove to the beach. It was a cool day and there were few people in sight. But the afternoon sun warmed us as we walked towards the water. There, my aunt took off her shoes and rolled up her pants. My mom and I did the same.

I handed a container to my aunt. She pried off the top and tilted it into the sea. My cousin's ashes tumbled out. A gentle breeze pushed them away from shore and we watched as they floated with the waves. We didn't say much beyond, "I miss you, Tony," and "I love you so much." When the container was empty my aunt handed it back to me. She wiped her face with her sleeve and walked back to the car.

The drive home was somber. We had hoped the scenery, movement, and time with family would help. We hoped the scattering of the ashes would have been cathartic. But she only drifted farther away.

For almost two months I lived in her house, but eventually I needed to move home. The memories of Tony were too close. I couldn't get a handle on my grief; it hurt too much.

We continued to check on Judy every day until one afternoon she didn't answer. Even in the best of conditions my aunt was lazy about returning phone calls so we didn't panic immediately. But as hours passed into the evening Mom finally called the police to perform a wellness check.

She learned the police were already there. Friends and colleagues from her hospital had been trying desperately to reach her when she didn't show up for work. After leaving over twenty voicemails, they had called 911.

When the officers found her it first appeared like she had simply fallen asleep on her son's bed. But she had stolen two drugs from the hospital. One makes a person unconscious and the other stops their heart. Sometime that morning she had entered Tony's room and injected herself first with one and then the other.

Through the walls of my room, I heard my mom cry out, begging for it not to be true. Grief twisted her voice into something otherworldly. I collapsed onto my bed and felt raw. Like my skin was bleeding. Like I had no protection left. Like I would never feel good again.

Three days later, and five months after I had done it for my cousin, I sat in Saint Paul's Lutheran Church and said goodbye to someone I loved.

It shattered me. I had been a smart kid. I graduated high school a semester early and had plans to go to college. But after this - first my best friend, then my second mother - I didn't give a shit anymore. All I wanted was to escape to a dark corner, no matter how dirty, and disappear.

Likewise the Spirit helps us in our weakness; for we do not know how to pray as we ought, but that very Spirit intercedes with sighs too deep for words.

- Romans 8:28

2003

The Lord is my shepherd; I shall not want. He makes me to lie down in green pastures; He leads me beside the still waters. He restores my soul; He leads me in the paths of righteousness for His name's sake. **Yea, though I walk through the valley of the shadow of death,** I will fear no evil; For You are with me; Your rod and Your staff, they comfort me. You prepare a table before me in the presence of my enemies; You anoint my head with oil; My cup runs over. Surely goodness and mercy shall follow me all the days of my life; And I will dwell in the house of the Lord. Forever. The Lord is my shepherd; I shall not want. He makes me to lie down in green pastures; He leads me beside the still waters. He restores my soul; He leads me in the paths of righteousness for His name's sake. Yea, though I walk through the valley of the shadow of death, I will fear no evil; For You are with me; Your rod and Your staff, they comfort me. You prepare a table before me in the presence of my enemies; You anoint my head with oil; My cup runs over. Surely

Not in the Head

My eyes opened in the darkness. Confused, I swung my legs out of bed then stepped carefully across my room; my feet were bare and the floor was messy. In the living room, thin blue lights from the DVD player helped me avoid stumbling into the coffee table. The house was perfectly quiet, then the doorbell rang again.

Others were home - my mom for sure - but no one else stirred. I reached for the door handle, but I already knew who was on the other side: my cousin, Tony.

He smiled at me from the porch. I knew he was dead but it didn't bother me. He laughed at the surprised look on my face and I felt lighter than I had in months.

"Schmidty," he said, "let's go for a ride."

I followed him out to his '81 Oldsmobile granny car. It had become mine since the funeral, a graduation present from my mom, but Tony climbed behind the wheel. He backed down the driveway and drove us down the quiet country road. Our conversation was easy, natural. We remembered things that happened when we were children. He asked after a girl he had dated. He made a couple jokes only I would find funny.

At the highway he turned south. There were no other cars. His voice was soothing as was the rumble of the tires over the pavement. We slowed to a stop at an intersection. To our left the road twisted through the bluff and disappeared deeper into Wisconsin. Straight ahead it winded along the Mississippi. To our right, over the bridge, was Red Wing.

"Ben," Tony said. The engine hummed underneath us. There was no moon, no light beyond the glow of the dash, but I could see him perfectly. "Listen to me," he said. He turned his head towards me and stared unblinking. "Everything is going to be all right."

I nodded in the darkness, feeling for the moment perfectly at peace.

The next moment, I woke up. The afternoon sun angled around the blinds as I rubbed at my face and rolled onto my side. Grieving people often have vivid dreams of the person they lost. I didn't attach any spiritual significance to it, even in those first moments of waking up, but I did feel better than I had since before he died.

A few hours later I carried the good feeling - it was something like hope - with me to Josh's house. Josh and I grew up going to mass together, but he was going through a rough time. Eventually he would clean himself up, go to college, get a great job in IT, but when he was eighteen he had a serious meth addiction.

The sun hung low in the sky, but Josh had pulled thick drapes across the windows, casting the room into darkness. Several people lounged in a rough circle, some on a tattered couch; one woman perched on an end table; a couple leaned against the wall. They sat too close and talked too fast. It was a room full of tweakers, each lit up on drugs and eager to see a new face.

I sat on the edge of the couch with Josh next to me on a folding chair. A man to my right took a deep drag off a pipe. His head had been shaved close, almost bald, with fresh red bumps at its base. He was a little guy, but wiry. Veins in his neck pulsed as he held his breath. He exhaled loudly then offered me a smoke.

I was still buzzing from the dream. Everything was going to be all right, Tony had said. He was fine. I was fine. It would all turn out okay. I grabbed the pipe. A green swirl cut through the clear glass. A wisp of smoke drifted from a hole at the tip. I had never smoked meth - sometimes called speed, we usually called it glass. I knew it was dangerous, but I was more curious than afraid. Before I could do anything, however, the front door exploded.

Four screaming men burst into the room wearing black clothes and hats. Their faces were exposed but I didn't know any of them. The skinny guy in front screamed louder than the others. His eyes were wide and spit flew from his mouth with every word. "Someone here," he said, "ripped off my brother." He talked too fast without taking enough breath. "One of you fuckers stole $200."

The man slapped his forehead, ran his hand down

his face, then pulled a gun from a jacket pocket. Sweat soaked into his shirt. He acted crazy high, and ready to shoot someone.

Every muscle in my body clenched so for a moment I couldn't move. *Don't let it hit me in the head.* Looking back, I have no idea why that was important, as if getting shot in the neck or chest wouldn't be as bad, but for a long panicky moment it was my only thought. *Not in the head. Please don't shoot me in the head.*

The bald guy who had offered me the pipe leapt up and screamed back. "Fuck off out of here!" He shoved the man with the gun in the chest.

The man stumbled back as his friends shouted, but he caught his balance before he fell. His face grew blank and he raised the gun a foot away from my face.

Not in the head! I thought.

The bald guy said, "Put that thing away!"

"Sit your ass down or go get my money."

"Nah, motherfucker. Pussy like you? You won't shoot."

The man with the gun jerked it back to cock it. The bald guy laughed, then, eyes bulging, he leaned forward and licked the end of the barrel. His buddies from the house jeered. I took a step back towards the wall. The man squeezed the trigger, but someone shoved him and his hand went wild. The gun fired inches from my face.

My ears rang. I furiously patted my chest, my neck, looking for the bloom of blood expanding across my shirt. Next to me Josh did the same, but we were both fine. The bullet had thunked harmlessly into the wall.

The room erupted with elbows and fists, the two groups shoving and punching whatever was nearest to them. They kicked over a lamp and smashed a boot through the glass coffee table. The bald guy lunged for the man with the gun and wrestled him out the front door.

It wasn't my fight - I knew no one besides Josh and he disappeared into a back room - so as soon as a path cleared, I got out.

Back in my cousin's old car, I sped home. Night had fallen and the world turned dark. My head hurt. An idiot with a gun shattered any lingering peace I had from the dream and left me feeling nauseous. It seemed everything good died while everything shit stuck around.

I stopped at the same intersection from my dream. No cars came from either direction and I idled there, a terrible numbness filling my chest. I missed my cousin. I missed my aunt. I wanted to go back to a time when the world made sense.

I couldn't stand feeling this way any more. I thought of the weight of the pipe in my hand, its delicate smoke. I wished I had taken a hit.

"And forgive us our debts, as we also have forgiven our debtors. And lead us not into temptation, but deliver us from the evil one."

                                        - Matthew 6:12-13

The Garage

It had been months since I had seen my brother. The last time he showed up at our mom's house I noticed his eyes had sunken into his cheeks, the skin on his face had coarsened, and his shirt hung loosely off his shoulders. He was on a path towards self destruction and I had wanted nothing to do with it.

But after the crazy man shot at me, my thinking changed. I was seventeen and hated waking up in the morning. I was sick of sadness, sick of the numbness, sick of all of it. I had been ignoring his calls - he was always looking for a ride - but finally, when his name showed up on my phone, I answered.

"Hey dumbass," he said. "I need a ride."

"Yeah?" I said. "Where to?"

"Come pick me up. I'm at Micah's."

"Micah? You serious?"

Micah was Alyssa's big brother. He was different than

the guys Jesse usually hung out with. Quieter. Usually
kept to himself. As far as I knew, the two had never
been friends.

"Just get over here. We're in the garage."

With that he hung up on me. It had been an irritat-
ing conversation, but curiosity mixed with something
darker compelled me to pull my cousin's car around.

As I rumbled up the driveway I twisted my neck to
search around the side of the house for Alyssa's car, but
it wasn't there. I couldn't imagine her hanging out with
my brother, but we had lost touch since Tony's funeral
and I wasn't even sure where she was living. I realized
as I parked how many friends had drifted away over
the past several months. I sat for a long moment feeling
very alone. Then, disgusted with myself, I kicked open
the door and spit.

My whole body ached as I climbed out of the car.
The house was bordered by corn fields on two sides
with the garage on the far end of the yard. I had never
known Alyssa's family to use it. It looked abandoned; it
had no windows, and the roof sagged. I approached it
cautiously and listened for a moment at the side door
before deciding to knock.

A woman I didn't know opened the door. A streak of
sun landed hard on her face and she blinked at it before
allowing me to enter. A few steps in, she closed the door
behind me, shutting out the daylight. Two naked bulbs
mounted on the ceiling cast a dim glow. Through the
dust I saw my brother slouched in an old lawn chair;
his buddy Derek perched on a stool. A large water bong
sat on a low table in front of them. Only when I drew

closer did I see Micah, huddled a few feet back in the shadows. Around them I smelled something like gasoline but sweeter and more musty.

Derek jerked his head in my direction. "What's he doing here, Jess?"

"It's fine," my brother said. "I called him."

Derek scowled, "What the hell?"

"It's fine. He's cool. Here." My brother passed the bong to Derek. He placed his lips against the glass and it swirled with smoke.

"Is that speed?" I asked but no one answered. When people smoked speed - also known as glass or meth - there is constant chatter; everyone sharing their big ideas, usually to get money or more drugs. It's all bull shit all the time at high speed. Everyone talking, no one listening. So I had to say it again to get their attention.

"What is that? Speed?"

Jesse said, "What do you think?"

"What's it like?"

"It's all right. Makes you kind of hyper."

My brother leaned forward to the table and removed an attachment from the base of the bong. He picked a crystal shard from a piece of paper and placed it gently in a round piece of glass with a hole on top. He fitted the attachment back into place and dug a lighter from his pocket. He gestured for me to lean in.

Glass. Highly addictive. Scars your skin. Loosens your teeth. Damages your brain. I knew all this. All around a bad idea, but I didn't give a shit. I reached for the bong and for the first time in weeks I didn't feel numb. I pressed my lips into the opening at the top, and, when the smoke gathered, I took a deep breath.

The smoke tasted sharp with a hint of something like gasoline. It was harsh, but I would grow to like it as an alcoholic likes the way liquor burns the back of his throat. I held my breath for several seconds and my eyes flicked over and caught Micah's gaze. In his face I caught a shadow of his sister. The first time I smoked pot I had called Alyssa and told her all about it, but I knew I'd never tell her about this.

Derek growled at me. "You smoking my shit?"

"He's just having a taste," Jesse said.

"A taste of my shit." He stared at me with dead eyes.

"It's as much mine as yours."

"Little fucker." Derek snatched the bong from me and spit on the floor.

I leaned back, and it wasn't long before I felt a low pleasant buzz - nothing too intense, a mild distraction for an afternoon. I experienced no side effects except my stomach cramped a bit. Glass, I'd learn, dries a person out.

They passed the bong around but Jesse didn't offer a second hit; he didn't seem to remember I was there. Derek kept glaring at me sideways as he rambled out a scheme to steal a car. Since neither had slept for three days, the scene only deteriorated from there.

"I'm gonna head out," I said, but no one looked up to notice. If my brother had really needed a ride somewhere he didn't mention it as I left.

Back in the sunshine, I felt good; oddly proud of myself. I had smoked glass but didn't lose my mind. I dabbled in hardcore drugs without any problems. It was a beautiful day. My thoughts were sharp. I started planning out my summer, some great ideas popping into my head as I sank into my cousin's car and pulled away.

When I got home I drank a large cup of water. The glass had made me thirsty but gave me no other trouble. The rest of the day was unremarkable and the next morning I woke up fine. My teeth didn't fall out. My face was unscarred. I smiled into the mirror. I was a badass, smoking glass couldn't hurt me at all.

Be alert and of sober mind. Your enemy the devil prowls around like a roaring lion looking for someone to devour.   *- 1 Peter 5:8*

The Dude

A figure lurched from the darkness of a back hall-way. A man. A giant. His face was in shadow except his wide eyes glowed perfectly white - no iris, just an inky dot in the middle.

The floor wobbled. My throat seized up. The night-mare towered over me. I struggled to breathe, but kept my face relaxed and lowered my shoulders. I neither flinched nor groaned. I blinked slowly and nodded.

My brother offered a half-assed introduction. He said the man's name was Fin.

He had me by a half a foot and seemed four-foot wide across the shoulders. He said, "You the little brother?"

"Yeah," I said.

He stared through me. To my brother he said, "He's all right?"

Jesse nodded. He had invited me and was known enough to vouch that I wouldn't run to the cops.

Fin settled into the couch next to the woman who owned the house, and picked a pipe off the floor. He dropped a giant crystal into it; easily $50 of high quality glass. This stuff wasn't made in the basement of some trailer park. It was made in a lab, probably in Mexico. He dug a torch lighter out of his pocket and started heating the bottom, careful not to let the flame touch the crystal as it would easily catch fire.

He shifted his face and I could see he was wearing special contacts to make his eyes glow white in the black light. He had wanted to scare me and it had worked; he remains the scariest human I have ever met. But I had fallen back on a skill which would prove useful throughout the next six years: no matter how freaky the situation, I could stay calm or at least fake it. Apparently, I had impressed him. After he took a long pull from the pipe, he offered it to me.

Less than a week had passed since I tried it in Alyssa's garage. Six numb days of going through the motions of life. Without another thought, I placed the warm metal to my lips and sucked in the smoke. I passed it to my brother. When the pipe made it back to Fin, he dropped in another crystal, took another hit then passed back towards me.

I took another hit and a strobe light exploded in my brain. With it came a rush, a euphoria, a feeling of power and ability. My brain, my senses all cranked up to 11. I was focused and brilliant. Ten thoughts raced around at the same time, all of them good, most close to genius. I was in control of my world. I was a god.

But I was a god who couldn't sit still. A chugging

momentum like a freight train pushed me forward. The others talked, spitting their ideas out on top of each other, but I couldn't follow the thread. I also couldn't control my eyes as they bounced around the room. It made me dizzy and a little nauseous. At the same time, I grew paranoid. The others were watching me, I could feel it. I respected these people - Fin especially - and wanted to impress them. If I couldn't fix my eyes they'd think I was a child who couldn't handle my drugs.

I forced my head down and focused on a dark stain about an inch away from my shoe. No one would think I was weird, I thought, as long as I sat perfectly still and stared at the floor. I committed to it. Time grew fuzzy, but twenty or thirty minutes passed with me this way: rigid, wide-eyed and silent. Finally, Fin said, "Hey, little brother."

I glanced at him but his white eyes freaked me out so I looked away.

"How much money you got?"

I told him I had fifty bucks in my wallet.

"Give it here."

I did without thinking. In return he gave me a plastic packet with two large tan crystals in it.

"Sweet," I said. "Thanks."

"Now get out of here. Let me know when you get more money."

I had been dismissed. I tucked the packet into a pocket and stood up. I felt a little dizzy, but had no problems making my way outside. On the porch, standing in the sunlight, middle of my little town, the freight train kept chugging and my mind kept pushing forward. It was a thrill: all energy, all momentum. I needed to move so I hopped in the car and took off. I drove in loping circles, not stopping until midnight when I almost ran out of gas. I went home and spent five hours pacing my room.

In the morning my head hurt and my stomach cramped. I needed water, food and rest. But in the pocket of my jeans I had a bag of glass which I thought was worth $50.

I called a friend. When I left the house I made a point to say good morning to my mom, giving her the impression I was up early and being productive. But ten minutes later in my buddy's garage I broke off a shard of glass and we smoked it. The next day we followed the same pattern. I was out of my room before seven to greet my mom then off to a garage to smoke dope. For three days we jabbered and fidgeted. We paced cramped rooms and drove around for hours. Piercing pains shot behind my eyes, through my back and chest, but the train kept pushing. Every time it started to slow down I'd quickly take more. I stopped sleeping but didn't care. Sure, glass made my body feel like hell, but at least I felt something.

I smoked half the weight Fin gave me, but the other half I decided to sell to a couple guys from school. A few months before I had watched them smoke crank off a piece of tinfoil at a party. They melted it with a lighter until it released a thin smoke which they sucked from the air with straws. At the time it seemed gross and stupid dangerous, a good way to kill themselves. But now I sat in my car - my leg bouncing, hands slapping at the wheel, the drug shoving me forward - and called them to offer the rest of the glass for $50.

Twenty minutes later we met up and I made my first sale of a hard-core narcotic. Five minutes after that I was on the phone to Fin, looking for more.

"Little brother," he said. "You got some money?"

I told him I got $50 for the stuff he had given me.

"That's all you got?" He laughed. "That shit was worth $300."

I froze up. I had made a huge mistake and for a moment I couldn't speak. "Ah hell, Fin. I didn't know. I thought it was fifty."

"Slow down, bro. No worries."

He laughed again and I relaxed. I thought he was being kind, but he was grooming me to be one of his dealers. The guys he had selling for him were all in their twenties. I was eighteen and could target a younger customer.

"Come on over," he said, "and we'll figure something out."

I raced over, eager to get started. Fin was feared and respected. He took no crap from anyone. He was smart and hustled a product for serious money. He was The Dude. Though based in the Twin Cities he spent most of his time in Red Wing and almost all of the drugs in the area - especially the high quality stuff - came through him.

I'd discover he had a peculiar moral code. He wouldn't sell to anyone under the age of eighteen. He would't sell to anyone going into or returning from rehab. He'd bail out his associates. He wouldn't nickel and dime his customers. Some of his rules were practical, but mostly they were a way to justify his business. He believed he was being ethical in an unethical world, and I bought into it. All the admiration I once had for my brother I transferred to Fin.

Within a week of meeting him, I became a low level drug dealer and started making what I thought was easy money. I planned to do it for a couple months. I was enrolled in business college in the fall and would stop using and selling before classes started. I'd make some repairs on my cousin's old car, fix it up nice, put a little money in the bank then be done.

No big deal.

Do not be deceived: God cannot be mocked. A man reaps what he sows. Whoever sows to please their flesh, from the flesh will reap destruction; whoever sows to please the Spirit, from the Spirit will reap eternal life.
- Galatians 6:7-8

Woof

I paid no attention to the cornfields as they whipped by. I ignored the phone ringing in the passenger seat. I simply drove. I needed the movement. I needed to be in my cousin's car with no particular place to go.

At a T intersection, I listened to the message; it was from my mom. We had a therapist appointment scheduled in thirty minutes. Her voice was hesitant, too soft, pleading.

It would be our second visit. Two weeks before she had poked her head into my bedroom.

"You got a minute?"

It was late morning. I had just woken up after a few hours of sleep. I was uncomfortably sober and my body hurt. I shrugged.

She leaned against the doorframe. "I'm worried about you."

She was right to be worried. I hadn't gone a day without glass since I first met Fin. It had only been three weeks but even high I knew something had broken inside me.

"I think we should go see someone. A therapist."

I was impossibly thirsty. Three people had just texted me looking to buy drugs. I was jonesing for a hit myself. But I hated the look on my mom's face so I nodded.

"Thank you," she said.

Two days later I followed her into a therapist's office. The counselor, a kind-eyed man with a deeply lined face, invited us to sit on his couch. A window allowed a bare slant of sunshine to fall across my legs. The man had offered me a Coke and I sipped at it as he chatted with my mom.

On the way there I had felt hopeful. I was a mess and maybe this guy could help. But when the counselor turned his attention to me some deep instinct rose up to fight.

"So Ben, tell me a little about yourself."

I shrugged then gave him a three word answer. He said something else and I folded my arms and lowered my chin to my chest. His questions were light, but I knew where he was heading. I sank deeper into the couch. I muttered every answer, barely giving a yes or no.

After an hour of this, we left. Mom didn't say a word as we drove home. In the driveway she placed the car in park but didn't shut it off.

"Ben," she had said when I reached for the door. "Would you be willing to try again?"

I'd never go back but I had a few hits of glass waiting for me and I wanted to get to them as quickly as I could.

"Ben?"

"Sure," I said.

Ten days had passed and, according to my mom's voicemail, our second appointment was in twenty-five minutes. I pulled a lazy U-turn to head back towards Red Wing. I drove north along the river, tapping a beat against the steering wheel. I hit the city limits and cruised down main street. Ten minutes before the appointment I approached the therapist's office. I passed with barely a flicker of guilt, turned at the next side street and followed it to the house Fin used as a base of operations.

I stepped in without knocking and the big man greeted me with a nod. The windows were blacked out and it was a relief to sit in the darkness. I wasn't in a cramped office having an uncomfortable conversation with a stranger. I was among friends. And, more important, I was about to get high.

"Little brother," Fin said, "I've got a problem."

I leaned forward. I had taken a long hit from the pipe and had forgotten all about my mom and the therapist. My thoughts were charged up and I was ready to help. I was addicted to the drugs, of course, but also to the hustle. Two other guys sat smoking with us. They both looked like men who had seen some action, done serious drugs, spent time in prison. Me, I looked like a child. I bleached my hair and the glass hadn't yet hollowed me out. I needed to earn my stripes.

I said, "What do you need?"

"You know this dude, Derek?"

A familiar lump settled in my gut.

"Derek owes me money," Fin said. This was no surprise. "But he was bragging here about these subs he's got."

"Yeah," I said, "I'd heard." Derek always drove a shitty car, but recently he had been showing off expensive - and probably stolen - subwoofers in the trunk.

Fin leaned back against the couch and rubbed a hand down his face. He looked for a moment like a tired old man. "I need you to go get them."

"The subs?"

"Yeah."

"From his trunk?"

He cut a glance at me out of the corner of his eye. "Yeah," he said. "Out of the man's trunk."

I blinked a few times, trying to process Fin's words. Derek was a monster, a bully, and something about me brought out the worst in him. I was a bean pole: a buck fifty and 6'4". He had a hundred pounds on me easy. And I'd seen him fight; he was brutal. In short, he'd rip me apart. It would be stupid for me to be the one to collect the subwoofers.

"I'll do it," I said. Stupid or not, I had just smoked a ton of dope.

Fin shrugged, the others said nothing, and I hurried out. The afternoon had drained into a quiet night. I took my car, although Derek's house sat on a corner only a few blocks from Fin's. Televisions and kitchen lights glowed through the windows on both sides of the empty street - normal people resting after a day of work - but Derek's house was perfectly dark. I eyed his car, parked against the curb at an aggressive angle, and pulled up behind it.

I took a deep breath. Time to move. I've always been one for the direct approach so I went straight to the front door and knocked. The glass buzzing in my head made me alert and gave me a nice buffer from the fear I should have been feeling. I was going to do this: face down a monster and prove myself to the boss.

Derek pulled open the door and I said, "I'm here for Fin."

"Benny?" For a moment he looked confused, then he smirked down at me. "He's not here."

"You owe him, he said."

He lost the smirk. "So?"

"So I've got to take your subs."

His face darkened. "What the fuck is this?"

I forced myself to stay calm. "Your subwoofers, D. He told me to come get them. Fin did."

"What the fuck, dude?" With each word he slammed his palm hard against the door frame.

I didn't flinch. I lowered my voice and grew quieter. "Until you pay Fin, he's gonna need to keep the subs."

Derek grew an extra inch and the muscles in his face and neck twisted into knots. I blinked and breathed. I didn't trust myself to speak but didn't look away.

"Shit." He yanked out his phone and pushed it to his ear. "You better not be screwing with me…" Talking with Fin his voice softened. "Hey yeah… I got Ben here and…" A word from the boss and he deflated. "Yeah…"

His shoulders slumped forward and now I had to

keep myself from smiling.

Derek stared at his phone. "All right, Schmidty, let's do this." Head down, defeated, he led me to his car and opened the trunk. It didn't take long; he unhooked a couple wires connected to two fat grey boxes. They were high quality, probably worth a thousand dollars if he paid for them. When I leaned in for one, he stopped me. "Nah shit, let me do it." He cradled each like an infant and placed them gently in my back seat. He didn't look at me as I got in my car and drove away.

Back at the house I set the subwoofers on the coffee table in front of Fin, like an offering. He glanced at them; didn't acknowledge me, but instructed another guy to carry them to a back room. I waited to see if I'd get a little weight for my trouble, but nothing was offered. It didn't bother me. I left soon after and stood outside my car. Nothing could bother me that night.

I had defeated a monster. I was king of the hill. I wasn't Jess's little brother any more.

I worked for Fin.

"I am the good shepherd. The good shepherd lays down his life for the sheep. The hired hand is not the shepherd and does not own the sheep. So when he sees the wolf coming, he abandons the sheep and runs away. Then the wolf attacks the flock and scatters it."

- John 10:11-12

2003-2005

The Lord is my shepherd; I shall not want. He makes me to lie down in green pastures; He leads me beside the still waters. He restores my soul; He leads me in the paths of righteousness for His name's sake. Yea, though I walk through the valley of the shadow of death, I will fear no evil; For You are with me; Your rod and Your staff, they comfort me. You prepare a table before me in the presence of my enemies; You anoint my head with oil; My cup runs over. Surely goodness and mercy shall follow me all the days of my life; And I will dwell in the house of the Lord. Forever. The Lord is my shepherd; I shall not want. He makes me to lie down in green pastures; He leads me beside the still waters. He restores my soul; He leads me in the paths of righteousness for His name's sake. Yea, though I walk through the valley of the shadow of death, I will fear no evil; For You are with me; Your rod and Your staff, they comfort me. You prepare a table before me in the presence of my enemies; You anoint my head with oil; My cup runs over. Surely

The Envelope

I threw the duffle bag in the trunk, and moved around the car; the door handle was still warm from the day. I started to blink then kept my eyes closed. I hadn't spent a day without smoking dope since meeting Fin. I leaned back against the car. Weeks, then months had passed in a blur and there I was, picking shit up for Fin and moving it around. An errand boy. A drug addict.

I opened my eyes. Disoriented, like I woke up from a bizarre dream. How long had it been? Two months? Three? I closed my eyes again and tried to remember. Time had grown blurry, slowed down to a crawl. I barely slept. I lost weight I didn't have to lose. Everything hurt all the time.

Something was terribly wrong. I had started college classes in the fall, but… I tried to piece together what month it was. I hadn't been to class in weeks. Instead I was in a gang neighborhood in Saint Paul with a bag full of something - drugs, guns, cash, I didn't know - in my trunk.

I needed time to think. My life had gone to hell but if I could take a step back and figure out how I got there I could start making it right; put myself back together. First thing: I needed to take a break. That had to be step one. Stop taking speed for a few days, and clear my head. I was a little high but when I sobered up I'd take a break. I'd get some sleep. I'd eat something, for God's sake.

My phone buzzed: Fin's name on the display. I stopped thinking and answered.

"Where are you?" His voice was heavy.

"Just got your bag."

"You need to make a stop on your way back." He directed me to a gas station in a nearby town. "Talk to Carol. She owes me."

"What do you want me to do?"

"Get my money."

"How?"

"Just get the envelope." He hung up.

I climbed into the car. Fin's project - get the envelope - immediately sucked all my attention. Glass did that; it helped me focus so all other thoughts, including me taking a break, were shoved to the side. The tires sprayed gravel as I hurried out of the parking lot. My brain cranked up so I muttered ideas to myself as I changed lanes, as I took an exit. I imagined the gas station and feverishly considered a dozen scenarios, evaluating my response to each. I thought through how I would act and what I would say when I confronted this woman, Carol.

Twenty-five minutes later I pulled into the gas station. Instinctively I stopped at a pump with the front of my car facing the exit. It had become habit. If something went wrong I didn't want to pull a U-turn in a narrow parking lot.

The humid night air poured in when I opened my door. I checked my surroundings. There was no one getting gas and only one car parked next to the building. Even the road, a main drag through town, was empty. It was late, after midnight, and the town felt abandoned.

The inside of the store was brightly lit. A classic rock station came muffled over the industrial hum of coolers and air conditioning. An older lady stood behind the counter, looking at me expectantly. There was no one else in the store. It was the perfect situation; everything was going my way.

An accidental prayer slipped out. Thank you, God. It had been an automatic response, a reflex from my catholic upbringing, and it shocked me. I was thanking God for what - for making it easy to intimidate a woman into giving me money? For helping my drug business go well? It made no sense.

Nothing I was doing made sense. I needed to stop. Step away for awhile. Figure this out.

"Can I help you?" The lady gave me the thin smile of a person sick of the service industry.

Dammit. I couldn't stop when there was work to do. I shook off the prayer as best I could. "I'm looking for Carol."

Her smile disappeared. From across the store, she

seemed put together. But as I stepped closer I saw her face had turned skeletal. Leathery skin stretched tight over her chin and cheek bones. Red lipstick had been smeared over dry lips.

"Who are you?" she said. Her eyes were empty.

"Are you Carol?"

A shrug.

"You owe Fin money."

She snorted. "I don't know what you're talking about."

"You owe Fin money. I'm here for an envelope."

"Who the hell are you?"

I was a just-turned-eighteen skinny white kid. I was an errand boy. I was a drug addict. I was nobody. "I'm Ben." I put a hard edge into my voice. "I work for Fin."

"Well Ben, I'm not giving you shit."

"Carol, listen." I gave her a dead-eye stare I had been working on. "You don't want me to have to come back. And you sure as hell don't want Fin to come out here."

The woman tapped a fingernail. I heard the sound of a truck passing but didn't look away.

She lowered her eyes. "Well shit," she said.

I was a kid. There was no way I intimidated the lady, but it didn't matter; nobody wanted to mess with my boss.

She ducked behind the counter. After some rummaging she produced an envelope. The corners were wrinkled, the edges soft: it had clearly been passed back and forth a few times. I reached for it, but she snatched it back.

I almost started laughing. "You have to give me that."

"Just wait." She grabbed a marker from next to the

register, the one they used to check if a bill is counterfeit, and traced along the seal of the envelope. Ten years later I still don't know what she was thinking. It must not have occurred to her how easy it would be to get a new envelope and a blue marker. But then, like me, she was probably pretty high.

Driving home I again felt stirred to pray. Everything had gone perfectly, and I had passed another test - collecting from a stranger. It had felt good, staring down the woman, placing the envelope in my back pocket, walking out into the night. I could put the envelope in front of Fin, and show him I was capable of handling more responsibility; a bigger stake in the business.

Some part of me wanted to give thanks.

But that made no sense. I was a drug dealer. I poisoned my community. I did bad things. God had no place in my world.

I tried to shake off the thought, but it nagged me the entire drive. Finally I parked outside of Fin's house and decided - for real this time - I needed to stop, at least for awhile. Clear my head. Figure this out.

I entered his living room jittery. Fin sat smoking on the couch. His eyes half closed, he barely nodded when I tossed the envelope in front of him. I stared for a moment at nothing, hand on the back of a chair, trying to remember the last time I had taken a shower. I scratched the back of my head; it had been a few days. I was grimy. My stomach hurt and I needed to drink some water. It was time to go home.

I turned to leave but was stopped by four men stumbling through the front door. I didn't know them. I assumed they had come down from the cities, and, like me, they did things for Fin. They were older. Their faces were scarred by old fist fights and recent drug use.

With a series of thuds they dropped a half-dozen lock boxes on the coffee table - and instead of leaving I sat down to watch, curious. They had a couple hammers, a screwdriver and a chisel. One guy used a kitchen knife. They started chipping at the locks.

The boxes came from a car dealership. It would take about an hour but once they got them open they would take the keys back to the dealer and take off with new cars. Once started, they would have a narrow window to get them to a garage in Minneapolis before OnStar kicked in.

It was a major crime, grand theft. If caught it could mean prison time, and by being in the room I had become part of it. This was the world I had chosen. But enough. I was done. I leaned forward, ready to move.

But then Fin lit a bong. The smoke billowed up and I figured I could hang out for a few more minutes. He passed it to me and I figured a hit of glass would help me think. A good smoke would clear my head so I could get a better handle on what happened to my life. After this I'd sit down for real and work out how to make it better.

I sucked in the glass and held my breath...

...and I was a gangster. I was in charge of my own existence. I was winning. The guys took their keys out into the night, chattering to each other at high speed. Fin sat back smoking and I was amazed. It was insanely complicated. He had lookouts, drivers, lock-breakers -

all working together under a tight timeline. He set it up. He'd get all the profits and all he had to do now was sit back and get high.

Clarity, finally. The glass had cleared my head so I could see what I wanted.

In the underbelly of small towns there was a pyramid. The bottom 90% were addicts. They wanted to get high, and had no other ambitions. Above them were petty dealers, guys like me working for guys like Fin. They acquired some weight and sold it for money and favors. On top of this pile of shit was the boss. He had the contacts, supplied the product, knew the users and terrified everyone.

Fin was our boss, and he understood it all - the business, human nature, the angles and margins. He could have been a straight businessman - and it was all about the business for Fin. There were no gang rites or racial connections. There were no allegiances or loyalty oaths; nothing like that. He cared only about making money.

I took another long hit. The idiotic thoughts which had been messing with my head were gone. I wasn't going to stop. Stopping meant pain. No, I wanted to push forward, move up. I had to keep getting the man his envelopes, duffle bags, whatever he needed - because I wanted more hustle. I wanted more money. I wanted more drugs.

I wanted to be Fin.

Do nothing out of selfish ambition or vain conceit. Rather, in humility value others above yourselves, not looking to your own interests but each of you to the interests of the others.   - Philippians 2:4-5

Road Spikes

Weeks blurred into a screaming mush. Birthdays, summer, college plans, Halloween, Thanksgiving dinner: all forgotten. All spent thirsty, moving, rambling, never sleeping, always dry. Every day I huddled in the shadows of a dark house; its windows blacked out or the blinds pulled tight.

"Shit, Ben. I'm fucked."

It was a basement this time. My buddy Tank perched at the edge of the couch. He ran a hand through his hair, grabbed a handful and tugged. "I've got too much."

The house belonged to Tank's girlfriend. She was upstairs, probably sleeping.

"Calm down, Tank," I said.

"I'm so fucked. I've got too much shit." He tapped his fists against his legs. "I've got too much."

He had a bit of weight on him. Nothing extreme. Nothing more than I'd typically carry around, but he had been awake for days and was schizing out. In his head the cops were outside ready to bust him.

"You're fine," I said. "No one's coming. Take it easy."

But he couldn't calm down, or stop moving. A thin rug covered the concrete - inside bare, unfinished walls - and he started marching tight circles around its edge.

"Naw hell. I can't. I'm not going down for this." He tossed two bags of glass, both about as big as a sugar packet, on the old weight bench he used as a table. He picked one up, opened it and tapped the crystals into the center of a rolling paper we called a zigzag.

"What the hell, Tank? Put that shit away."

He wrapped the zigzag around the glass into a bundle about an inch square. I laughed nervously. There are four ways of taking glass: snort it, eat it, smoke it or inject it. Snorting and injecting were crazy and I tried eating it only once. Like Tank, I had wrapped it in rolling papers so it wouldn't cut or burn me on the way down. Then I waited for more than ten minutes for it to hit. When it did, it exploded too hard inside my brain and made me feel out of control. I'd never do it again.

Tank popped the bundle in his mouth and gulped.

"Holy shit, man. What are you doing?"

He grinned. Eyes too wide. "Just taking my medicine." He poured the second baggy on the paper and wrapped it up. He smacked his tongue loudly against the roof of his mouth. He swallowed another $50 worth of glass, this time washing it down with a rum and coke.

In the span of a few minutes, Tank ate as much glass as a serious addict would go through in four or five days, on top of whatever he had taken before. Stunned,

I sank back on the couch. I often told myself I took speed to help me think, but I'd gone blank.

He jabbered at me, piling words on top of words in a mix which made little sense. Several times I told him to calm himself, to slow down, but he ignored me.

After about ten minutes he raised his hand, palm side out, as if looking for a high five.

"Whoa. Ben?"

"Yeah?"

He slapped himself hard across the face. I leaned away from him, pushing myself into the cushion. Then he bent at the waist to scream red-faced at the floor and I flinched. When I looked back he was jerking his head like a dog with a rope. "Aw hell," he said and sprinted up the steps.

Light tumbled down from the upstairs kitchen as I stared up after him. I couldn't wrap my mind around what had just happened. Tank had never been a serious user. He wasn't part of the world like I was. He'd mess around with us on the occasional weekend but be sober for work on Monday. I had never seen him messed up like this.

I sprinted up the stairs, taking them three at a time. Glass turns a user's focus inward, keeping him from feeling empathy, but concern for my friend had pierced through the haze. In the kitchen, I called his name but he didn't answer. I searched through the rest of the main floor, but the house was quiet. I found no sign of him or his girlfriend.

I listened dully to the hum of the refrigerator. I watched headlights pass on the street outside. The clock on the microwave advanced a minute, but still no sign of Tank. I had no idea what to do, so I went with what I knew best.

Ten minutes later I was smoking with Fin in a dark living room. I took a long hit and my concern for Tank became a dull ache. A second hit and I had bigger things on my mind.

"Hey man." Whispers of smoke puffed from Fin's lips. "You got a pistol?"

I shook my head. I had a hunting rifle and a shotgun and told him so.

"All right, you got to get a throwaway." A throwaway was a stolen gun; it couldn't be traced. "I know a guy. Go talk to him." He took another long hit, holding it in his lungs as long as he could. He coughed into his fist, then nodded at my jacket. "That thing got a pocket?"

It was early December and cold outside, though I barely noticed. My jacket was thick, too warm, ill-fitting. But yeah, it had a pocket. I nodded and patted at my hip.

"Nah, inside. Up here." He tapped his fist against his chest.

"Yeah." It was a winter jacket; they all had them.

"All right, talk to my guy and get yourself a Kaltec 9, something small like that. Keep it in that pocket." He tapped his fist again to his chest. "And you keep that coat on you, all right? I don't care if you're sweating your balls off, you keep that coat on you. One with a little pocket up here. You got me?"

I got him. Get a jacket. Wear it all the time. Get a gun. Sweat my balls off.

"All right, now I need your help with something."
He closed his eyes and pinched at the ridge of skin between his eyes. He remains the scariest man I have ever
met but for a moment he looked like an annoyed high
school math teacher. "These dudes owe me."

Those dudes owed him about eight thousand dollars. It was a lot of money, but a fairly common part of
the life. An individual or small group would get some
weight from Fin to sell. They'd pay for some but he'd
front the rest. These guys would be addicts; they've got
to use, so they'd smoke a little themselves in the car.
They'd plan on calling their friends, but would use a bit
more that night. A week later the stash was gone and
they'd made nothing and owed Fin money. It would
spiral from there. They'd get fronted from someone
else, go through the same pattern and owe both. Most
dealers never function properly to make a dime; they'd
just dig themselves deeper, doing what they can to stay
high until they owe thousands of dollars to a man like
Fin.

Fin said, "I need you to meet up with the guys to see
about collecting."

It took a moment to understand what he said - this
was an invitation to sink deeper into the belly of the
beast. Fin had never before included me in this side
of the operation. I hadn't stolen anything or assaulted
anyone. I was too young, probably, and too scrawny for
him. That night, I don't know, maybe he was short a few
men, but I was getting called up to the big leagues.

I'd like to say I was conflicted. I'd like to say I wrung
my hands, stared into the night sky and wondered what

kind of man I wanted to be. But that would be a lie. No, I took a hit and the rush cranked me up, building to the force of a freight train. I leapt to my feet, ready to move.

I hurried to my granny car, ready to meet the guy about a gun and become a true badass, but was distracted by a phone call. Tank's name was on the screen. I had forgotten about him and his call was an annoyance; I had things to do. Still, he was one of the few friends I had left and I couldn't bring myself to ignore him.

He started in as soon as I answered the phone. "Ah fuck, Ben, fuck." He tried to whisper but talked too fast and slipped into shouting. It sounded weird as hell. "I just hit somebody."

I told him to calm down.

"I just ran someone down. I think he's dead. Aw shit."

"Take a breath, Tank. Tell me what happened."

"I don't remember."

"Where are you?"

"I'm in my house, Schmidty. In the bathroom."

"Okay. And where did this happen?"

"I don't. I can't remember."

"Where did you go?"

"I didn't."

"Tank."

"You were with me. You were in the basement with me."

"Tank?"

"Ah fuck, Schmidty. I'm in trouble."

"Tank, you're not making any sense. Did you leave the house?"

"No. It was in the basement. With you."

He had not run anyone over; he never even left his house. But he had lost connection with reality.

"You gotta come help me. You gotta get me out of this."

We had history. Tank had been a good friend and now he clearly needed help.

"Ben, you there?"

But Fin had invited me deeper into the organization. It was an opportunity for more hustle, more drugs, more respect. I had to show him what I could do.

"Schmidty?"

"Yeah," I said. "I'm here." I slammed my palm hard against the steering wheel. It felt like weakness but I couldn't turn my back on Tank. "I'll be right over." I hung up, spat out a curse and turned around. I had to move fast. I needed to find him, talk him down and get him into the care of his girlfriend. If I hurried, I could still get the gun from the guy before the meet up.

A little past the dinner hour, I drove through another perfectly ordinary neighborhood. Televisions glowed through living room windows. Silhouettes moved through kitchens. Streetlights flickered on around me - but Tank's house was black. The driveway cut sharply down from the garage. A car idled at the bottom, its back tires resting against the sidewalk. A shadow sat behind the wheel.

I climbed out of my car and peered into his. Tank nodded at me and rolled down the window.

"You going somewhere?"

"I don't…" his voice trailed off.

"How about we head inside."

He shook his head.

"I thought we could hang out."

"I gotta move, Schmidty."

"Where to?"

"To the moon, motherfucker."

"Easy."

"I gotta move." He put the car in gear and it jolted back a few inches.

"Whoa. Hold up. Let me drive."

"Naw," he clutched the wheel. "I got it."

I thought of Fin and his gun guy as I settled into the passenger seat. I gritted my teeth as Tank slowly drove away from the house. Screw it, there was nothing I could do, so I focused on my friend. As we hummed through the neighborhood he stayed in his lane, used his turn signals, and moved at a reasonable speed. Outside the car, he would have seemed fine. Inside, however, he was a mess. He couldn't sit still: his leg bouncing, shifting in his seat, leaning forward and back, adjusting his grip on the wheel, scratching at his hair, pulling at his ear. And he kept talking, but his words didn't make any sense.

He took us across the river into Wisconsin. We cut through farmland on empty country roads.

"Aw hell!" It was the first words I could understand since we left the house. "You see that?" He leaned forward, stared into the rearview mirror then swung his head around.

Behind us there was nothing but cornfields buried in snow. I said, "There's nothing there."

"Cops behind us."

"There's nobody there, Tank. You're fine."

"Okay." He sat back and seemed to relax. We were cruising at just below sixty miles an hour.

"Aw hell!" He slammed on the brakes. The wheels locked up, the car twisted on the pavement then skidded into the gravel shoulder. My head had snapped forward and the seatbelt cut into my neck.

"Road spikes!" He pointed towards a grove of trees. He saw cop cars, a roadblock, but there was nothing there.

I rubbed my neck and turned my head to the side. I'd be sore for days. "Tank, listen, you've got to let me drive."

"They're - we're fucked."

The tires spun through the gravel and he pulled us back onto the road. He drove, then kept driving, for the next three hours, taking me in giant circles around rural Wisconsin. The window to get the gun closed as we drove over a narrow bridge on a gravel road. At the time I was supposed to be meeting up with Fin we were driving slowly alongside a country cemetery.

Tank talked without making sense while I sulked in the passenger seat. Everything always worked against me. Some dark force kept fighting to keep me down. Maybe it was bad karma but it didn't seem fair. I wallowed in my self pity. I had my opportunity to impress the big guy and it had all gone wrong. It always went wrong.

It was well after midnight and we were almost out of gas when Tank pulled up to his girlfriend's house.

He was done driving finally and - without a word of goodbye or any acknowledgement that I was there - he disappeared back inside the house.

I screamed out in frustration. A friend was having some kind of psychotic episode behind the blackened glass of his house, but I was pissed off. I climbed into my own car, slamming the door behind me. Instead of impressing Fin I probably made him angry. Everything was screwed up.

I turned on my car, but I didn't know where to go. I'd often head home for a few hours after midnight, pace around my room until dawn and then leave after my mom woke up - I wanted her to think I was a functioning human being - but that night the drug chugged too hard through my system; it pushed me forward. Home wasn't an option and I was sick of driving around. Like always, there was only one place to go.

I arrived a few minutes later. Fin's house looked deserted, but I knocked anyway. I took a half step back when Derek opened the door. Behind him I was shocked to see Alyssa's brother Micah slouching on the couch.

I hadn't seen Micah for months, since the first time in the garage, but even in the dark I could tell he looked like hell. His face was red, his eyes raw and his hands were shaking.

I had a hard time looking at him. "Where's Fin?"

Derek said, "Here somewhere, I don't know. We just got back."

Micah was trying to fill a syringe with the glass they had melted on a piece of tin foil, but his fingers trembled too much to do it.

"Fin was asking for you." Derek grabbed the syringe out of Micah's hand. "Said you were supposed to be there." He filled the syringe, stared at it. Tapped it with his finger.

"He pissed?"

"Fuck if I know." He moved over next to Micah and grabbed his arm. He massaged the inner part of his elbow, peering at it for a moment until it spasmed. "Keep still, dip shit." Derek looked at me with a sick grin. "You missed it." He listed off some of the guys who were there. "We bust in like a SWAT team. Gathered all those assholes into a room. Tied them up with some zip ties. Then it got hardcore." He told me about how one of the guys in the house thought he was going to be executed and started to cry. Another spit at him and they beat him unconscious. Horror filled me as I listened; this wasn't what I wanted. It sounded like a nightmare but Derek laughed as he gripped Micah's arm. This time it stayed still. "We searched around and found all kinds of shit. Body armor, guns. Fuck, if they were ready for us, we'd have had a shoot out.

"That…" he trailed off as he focused on the needle. He brought it to Micah's arm and I flinched as he pushed it in. I tried hard not to think of Alyssa, of their parents, of my childhood.

Derek grinned up at me. "That," he said, "would've got messy."

For the Son of Man has come to seek and to save that which was lost.
                                        -Luke 19:10

The Butcher

"I need you to do something for me."

He wasn't asking but I said, "Sure Fin, what do you need?"

"I got to head to Chicago for a few days and need someone to look after things." Fin paused to look at his phone. I sat forward and tried not to look too eager.

"I need you to pick up a guy from Saint Paul."

I masked my disappointment with a nod.

"Dude's name is Roach."

I knew Roach; he was part of a Latino gang out of Saint Paul. My brother had introduced us. Generally gangs didn't associate with people outside their group, but they'd smoke with Jesse. He said it was because he had darker skin and black hair. This made him look Italian which was Latino enough for these guys.

One night a few months back Jesse had called me for a ride. I had nothing going on so I drove him up to

Saint Paul. It was after midnight, the streets were empty and I had been doing thirty down a residential street when Jesse pointed hard across my chest.

"Stop there!"

I hit the brakes and skidded to a stop. As I navigated the tight U-turn I slipped and hit the horn.

Jesse shouted, "What the hell?"

I ignored him.

"You just honked outside a gang house." He cursed. "In the middle of the night."

"It was an accident."

"It was stupid."

I shrugged him off and parked. The house looked deserted but my brother knocked, and after a few moments of fidgeting on the porch, the door creaked open. A man stood backlit in the entryway wearing what appeared to be an expensive mink coat. Acne scars pocked his face. His head was smooth and covered with tattoos. Along the base of his neck a gang symbol had been inked with the word "LORD" below it.

"Little brother," Jesse said. "Meet Roach."

I reached out my hand and he shook it limply. He invited us to smoke and it became another endless night.

That was two months ago. Now I said to Fin, "You got Roach watching after things while you're gone?"

"Yeah."

"When should I get him?"

He looked up at me like it was a dumb question and said, "Now."

An hour later I was invited into a different house owned by a St. Paul gang. It was noisy, full of people and music. From a back room I heard the muffled yapping of little dogs.

A man welcomed me in. He had sleepy eyes but grinned as if he were happy to see me. I was a nobody, an errand boy; the guy could have shot me in the back of the head and no one would blink - but I worked for Fin so it was cool.

I asked for Roach and the guy pointed me to a door behind the kitchen. I skirted around three men sitting at the table. One of them had a pistol disassembled in front of him. He rubbed a gray rag against a part hidden in his hand. None of them looked up.

I opened the door and the sound and smell of puppies tumbled out. A wire cage against the back wall held a litter of Chihuahuas. Roach, wearing the same mink coat, stood over them, grinning.

"Check out the puppies, man."

They were the ugliest animals I had ever seen. "Cute dogs," I said.

He lifted them one at a time, showed them to me. A hard-ass gang-banger, he scratched one behind the ear, scolding it when it nipped at his finger.

"You want to hold one?"

"Nah."

He glared at me a moment, then shrugged. "That's alright," he said and gently placed the one he was holding in it's cage. "Let's do it." He nodded to the door and followed me out into the kitchen.

"Hey kid, hold up," Roach said. "This is the Butcher." He gestured to the man who had been cleaning his gun. He was thick and bald, had no neck or tattoos. He held his head tilted towards the ground and didn't look at me.

"He's coming with."

"Fin didn't say anything about him."

Roach said, "That a problem?"

The Butcher stared up at me with dead eyes.

"Naw," I said. "No problem at all."

We stepped outside and a third person, a girl, followed us. She had been pretty, I could tell, but drugs had hardened her skin and pulled it tight against the bones in her face. Any sparkle she might have had in her eyes had drained away. No one introduced her to me - I never did learn her name - but she slid in the back seat next to Roach.

The Butcher rested a hand on the top of my car and pulled a pistol from the waistband of his jeans with the other. He leaned in and placed it on the floor directly behind me. Then he climbed in next to the girl.

Honestly, I was barely eighteen and the whole thing, the guns, the gang-life, The Butcher in the back seat, even those ugly-ass puppies, all of it made me feel like I was in total control of a deadly game.

I had never been the cool kid. I wasn't a great athlete. I got along okay with my classmates but often felt invisible. Now I was a badass, driving Roach and The Butcher through the city while my classmates were working part time jobs for minimum wage. As far as I could tell, I was winning.

Or so I thought - but then the girl moaned. I adjusted the rearview mirror and saw her slump back against the seat. Sweat beaded on her forehead. Her skin turned pale, almost green. She moaned again and louder.

I could guess what had happened. Roach needed to move drugs with him to Red Wing, and my '81 Oldsmobile was the kind of car a police officer might stop simply because it looked suspicious. One place a cop can't search on a routine stop: a body cavity, in this case the girl's vagina. At some point, probably while Roach and I played with the Chihuahua puppies, she took regular sandwich bags - the kind you buy at any grocery store - filled them with dope, tied them up with a rubber band and placed them inside herself.

She had done it for money or for drugs, or because she thought she was Roach's girlfriend, or she needed protection. I don't know exactly her motivation, but I know they were using her. This was not uncommon in that world. Men used women as things, containers, a layer of protection between themselves and the police. But in this case one of the bags must have torn, or the rubber band had loosened, and the drug was leaking into her body. By her reaction it probably wasn't glass, but heroin; a drug which would knock her out and eventually stop her heart.

We were about halfway to Red Wing, driving through a little river town. Behind me the men started arguing in Spanish.

I said, "Should we take her to the hospital?"

There was some muttering I couldn't quite hear.

"No," Roach said. "No hospitals. We got a place we will take her."

He directed me through a couple of side streets to another ordinary looking house in a nice neighborhood. They pulled the girl out of the car - she was barely conscious - and dismissed me. I don't know what happened to her next. Maybe they raced her to a doctor and she got the care she needed. Maybe they had somebody at the house who knew how to help.

But as I drove off and saw the way they half dragged her, the top of her feet sliding against the pavement, I felt a hollow sickness spread through my chest. They had used this girl as a thing and now she could die because of it. I was no innocent bystander. This was the world I had chosen.

I hurried home. I didn't feel like a badass any more. I didn't feel in control. It was all wrong. It was all dark. Something deep within me longed to cry out to God. I wanted to pray for the girl to be okay - and beg for forgiveness for myself - but I shoved it away. Prayer was a dangerous slope and I didn't like where it might lead.

No, it was much easier to get a little high and do my best to forget.

Have mercy on me, O God,
  according to your unfailing love;
according to your great compassion
  blot out my transgressions.
Wash away all my iniquity
  and cleanse me from my sin.
                    - Psalm 51:1-2

Chasing My Tail

A few hits of speed and your mind cranks up to its highest gear and keeps whining along through the night. You become preoccupied with cleaning your tennis shoes or ripping apart your dirt bike and forget little things like eating and drinking. Twenty hours later you haven't slept at all, your mind is foggy and your body aches everywhere; you want to go to bed, but you still have the drug in you which means you can't sleep. You want to feel better so you do the thing that makes sense only to an addict - you take another hit.

In this way the meth addict constantly chases his tail. Up for two days, he'd sleep for an hour, then be up for three days more. The drug would make him feel lousy so he'd take more drugs to feel better. He'd keep it up until eventually his whole system shuts down or he goes batshit crazy.

After meeting Roach and the Butcher, I did this for ten straight days.

The final afternoon of that stretch I saw Fin for the last time. Roughly once a week he would front me some weight. I'd get hundreds of dollars worth of product and he'd expect me to pay him later. Typically I'd use half of it, and sell the rest. As I've said, I was addicted to the hustle as much as to the drug so I worked at it and my customer base grew.

I made him good money, but Fin was in a pissy mood when I met him. After passing me the weight he nodded towards the door and said, "Get the fuck out." It was the last thing he'd say to me.

Outside the sun cast long shadows across the pavement. I rested my head against the top of the car and yawned. For ten days I had scrambled around, hustling drugs, wide awake; it was finally time to go home. I crossed the bridge into Wisconsin with heavy eyelids. Whether it was the hum of my cousin's car, the hypnotic effect of highway stripes, or simple biology, I don't know, but by the time I pulled into the driveway I could barely move. I stumbled across my yard, somehow made it to my bedroom and fell unconscious on my bed.

Twenty-six hours later my eyes opened. I struggled to move. Glass always dampened my appetite and lately food had started to taste funny, so I hadn't eaten for days. I desperately needed water. With every motion, screaming jolts of pain shot through my stomach, my head, every muscle, and every joint - yet I somehow crawled out of bed. The kitchen had been moved impossibly far away, but I made it. I didn't know the time but it was dark outside so I tried to be quiet as I shoved anything which didn't need to be cooked into my mouth: a bowl of cold cereal, a few cheese sticks, a granola bar.

The hall light flicked on and I stopped chewing. Through an exhausted haze I saw my sister studying me, clearly confused by my behavior.

"Ben? What are you doing?"

"I'm not feeling well."

She peered at me and I turned away. She was a few years younger than I was. Healthy. Smart. On a good path. Although my family knew I was having a hard time, speed kept me moving and away from the house. In the rare times they saw me, I appeared energetic, up early and out the door.

"I'm sick," I said. "The flu."

She pressed her hand against her lips. "It's so late."

I tried to ignore the fear in her voice. "Stomach ache," I said. "Excuse me." I stumbled by her into the hallway. Then I went to the bathroom. Then I went back to bed.

Besides one more trip to the kitchen and a couple to the bathroom, I slept for another full day. Almost fifty-four hours - two straight days - after I came home I finally woke up.

I rolled my legs out of bed and struggled to sit. Everything was pain. My neck spasmed. My brain throbbed against my skull. The smallest flicker of light made me wince. I regretted every decision I had ever made.

There sat the gangster, the badass, the hustler. If I make the mistake in any part of this story of glamorizing the life I was living, remember this image: a kid slumped on the edge of his bed, pasty white, skin on bones, holding his back like an old man, flinching away from the hall light.

It was all shadow, all darkness, all pain. I had made my choices, as shitty as they were, and there was no getting out. I knew only one way to cope with the mess I had made of my life.

I fumbled with my clothes, pausing for long breaks, exhausted from pulling up my pants. I stumbled to the kitchen. There, I crammed down whatever I could find, drank water, then stepped bleary-eyed into the morning. I drove a little way down the road to a quiet spot. It was risky out in the open but I couldn't wait. My fingers shook a little as I prepared the pipe, but that was all right. Soon everything would be okay. I took a hit and held the smoke in my lungs as long as I could.

Relief came, slow at first then enough to function. My brain rebooted so I could think again. The pain didn't go away; it never did, but it was covered over, submerged in the chugging engine of the glass.

I turned up the radio, my heart thumping in my chest, and scrolled through the messages on my phone. I had dozens from customers; I had been out two days and they had grown increasingly desperate, vicious even, for their fix. I started to respond, but a series of messages came in from the night before which shoved everything else to the background. They each said essentially the same thing: "Did you hear? Fin got picked up by the cops."

Do you not know that your bodies are temples of
the Holy Spirit, who is in you, whom you have received
from God? You are not your own; you were bought at a
price. Therefore honor God with your bodies.

                                    - 1 Corinthians 6:19-20

Thirst

Fin was a force of nature: ruthless, tough and unstoppable. I'd never have imagined anyone could take him down. Still, I felt nothing when I heard the news; some shock, sure, but no sadness. I had admired the man as a twisted mentor for almost a year, but I experienced no sense of loss when he was gone.

Of course, by that time I felt little of anything. I had disconnected with old friends. I had stopped seeing my family. I had no real affection for anyone. In the world of shadows, guns and drugs, there were only users and the used.

I heard eventually that they sent him to prison for years; he might still be there, I don't know. But Fin's arrest created a vacuum, so I felt his absence in one way: I needed a new source. It became a significant problem. A few dealers came down from the Cities to take his place but no one lasted more than a couple months:

some were arrested, some moved on. Because of this, the quality of the product moving through Red Wing was poor and the supply was inconsistent.

But I kept at it. I scrambled for reasonably priced weight to buy. Since I was easy-going, and comfortable talking with all kinds of people, my network had grown a lot over the course of the year I had hung with Fin. I worked my connections, but it wasn't fun. It wasn't cool or badass. It became a grind, a dull cycle of scratching out enough profit to stay high.

In this way I lost another year of my life, of which I remember almost nothing except an endless hunger for more.

Then Jesus declared, "I am the bread of life. Whoever comes to me will never go hungry, and whoever believes in me will never be thirsty."   - John 6:35

Bad Dream

Trees choked out the midday sun and cast dark shadows across my windshield. I followed the driveway as it twisted around a hill to the trailer home. The windows were dark, and the siding stained with rot in the places it hadn't fallen off. Bags of garbage sat on bare stretches of dirt near rusty car parts.

If Fin were still around he would have cursed at me. He had rules, remember, and even after he was gone I tried to keep them. For one, they allowed me to believe I was being ethical in an unethical world. I could think: I don't sell to a guy getting out of rehab so I'm not that bad. Having that boundary, as thin as it was, made the rest of it feel better.

But many of his rules were practical. He had no patience for broken windows or torn up lawns. These places drew attention. They announced to the cops: people are doing drugs here. If it looked like a crack house, he'd have nothing to do with it.

On my own, however, some of his rules, even the smartest ones, had to be broken. I needed to get the glass. To get the glass, I needed to make the sale. To make the sale, I needed to go inside this horror-movie trailer house.

The metal landing swayed with my weight. When I raised a fist to knock, a man yelled, "Door's unlocked."

I pushed the door open and the smell knocked me back. I had to take a moment and breathe through my mouth with a hand against my face, but it wasn't enough. The air was soupy. It made my eyes water and my stomach throb up into my chest.

A man slouched over a kitchen table where cans of chili rotted on top of a week-old pizza. He looked like one of the after posters in a 'Don't Do Drugs' PSA: rotten teeth, thin hair, skin covered with angry red burns. Around him, garbage of all kinds covered every surface about waist high.

The man was grinning at me, unembarrassed. He raised up a pipe and invited me for a smoke.

Generally I could relax in almost any situation and talk without judgement to anyone. This guy, however, and his house, had passed my limit. I had to take shallow breaths to keep from vomiting; sharing a smoke wasn't going to happen. Still, I needed the customer so I propped the outside door open with my foot and listened to him ramble.

He made something like a joke, and as he laughed I heard a rustling underneath an empty potato chip bag. The man stopped and together we watched a mouse skitter into view. It sniffed its way to what looked to be a month-old Stouffer's lasagna and started nibbling.

Something exploded. It was loud and close - a bright flash and boom that rattled the walls and made my ears ring. I scrambled back thinking maybe it was a gas line until I saw the guy aiming a .22. He fired again and a top layer of garbage burst into a cloud.

I pushed out the door, ears ringing, and sprinted to my car. I tore down the driveway and skidded onto the gravel road. Several miles later I finally slowed down, opened my window, breathed in some fresh air and started to laugh.

For awhile I told everyone about the crazy man shooting up his kitchen as a joke. Everyone found it funny, but the memory irritated me. I kept picturing the guy in my head: his scarred face, the toothless grin, the smell. It bothered me. I couldn't help worrying that he was my future. That could be me, if I lived long enough: a lunatic drowning in his own filth.

Weeks went by and the rest of it - the girl in the back seat, Micah shooting up with Derek, days spent in the shadows, nights pacing my room - it all became too heavy. Too dark. A waking nightmare.

One morning I woke up after an hour or two of sleep and ate a little breakfast. My head hurt and my stomach cramped. I checked my stash and discovered I didn't have any weight. I stared at the empty container, took a gulp of orange juice and decided not to go looking for more.

The day passed, then two, and I stayed sober. I start-ed sleeping again. Eating regularly. The headaches went away and my body felt better. My brain was foggy and slow but I could manage.

After a few weeks I figured I had made it out. My experience in the world of drugs had been a bad dream which would forever be behind me. I got lost for awhile but found my way back in one piece.

Honestly, I was proud of myself: I had done it without help. I broke the addictions through the sheer force of my own will.

And this, I'd find out, was why it didn't last.

Therefore, I urge you, brothers and sisters, in view of God's mercy, to offer your bodies as a living sacrifice, holy and pleasing to God - this is your true and proper worship. Do not conform to the pattern of this world, but be transformed by the renewing of your mind. Then you will be able to test and approve what God's will is - his good, pleasing and perfect will.

- Romans 12:1-2

2006-2008

The Lord is my shepherd; I shall not want. He makes me to lie down in green pastures; He leads me beside the still waters. He restores my soul; He leads me in the paths of righteousness for His name's sake. Yea, though I walk through the valley of the shadow of death, I will fear no evil; For You are with me; Your rod and Your staff, they comfort me. You prepare a table before me in the presence of my enemies; You anoint my head with oil; My cup runs over. Surely goodness and mercy shall follow me all the days of my life; And I will dwell in the house of the Lord. Forever. The Lord is my shepherd; I shall not want. He makes me to lie down in green pastures; He leads me beside the still waters. He restores my soul; He leads me in the paths of righteousness for His name's sake. Yea, though I walk through the valley of the shadow of death, I will fear no evil; For You are with me; Your rod and Your staff, they comfort me. You prepare a table before me in the presence of my enemies; You anoint my head with oil; My cup runs over. Surely

Slingshot

A thin smoke, slightly metallic, wafted up from the basement. I gently pulled the door closed until it clicked. Behind me the laughter and music, the sounds of a good party, became muffled. I followed the wooden steps down to the cement.

"Hey Ben," My brother sat on our old couch, grinning at me. Two guys sat with him. "Hell of a party you got here."

"Didn't think you'd make it," I said.

"Wouldn't miss it." With one hand he touched a pipe to his lips and with the other he flicked a lighter underneath the glass bowl. A moment later a cloud of smoke puffed from his mouth and nose. When he looked at me again, he laughed. "Oh shit." He raised the pipe. "Is this okay?"

I'd had a good year. I got a job at Sears. I had a girlfriend and we had moved together into a nice house.

I had reconnected with old friends - real friends, not users. I felt great. The world of glass and shadow was behind me.

I shrugged. "Yeah, go ahead."

He took another hit and passed it on. My girlfriend and I had invited him, all three of them, to our party. They meant no harm, or at least that is what I told myself. It was New Years Eve. This was their way of having fun.

One of my brother's friends extended the pipe towards me. "You want some?" He didn't know me well enough to know I was sober.

My eyes flicked to the pipe. To the fingers which held it. To my brother's face, turned away from mine. I had a good life. I liked my job. I could still remember the stomach cramps, the dryness, the endless hunger for the next hit. I knew it would be stupid to do anything besides tell them, "No thanks." And maybe, "Get the hell out of my house."

But I also remembered the rush, especially after that first smoke. It would hit my brain like a freight engine and jack me up. A dozens thoughts all at once. Power. Confidence. Like I could do anything.

It had been a good year, but my brain wasn't working quite right. I was spacey. I'd start a sentence, lose the thought halfway through and end by staring stupidly at my shoes.

And it hadn't been that great of a year. I still missed my cousin. My aunt. I tried not to think about them, to push those feelings away, but it took too much effort. Some stupid thing would remind me and the grief collapsed in so I couldn't breathe. And on top of that I had this new emotion: shame. I didn't know how to process it after two years of poisoning my community with drugs.

I didn't want to become an addict again. I didn't want to sell drugs. I didn't want to lose what I had, but... some distance from my emotions, a little cushion for even a few hours? I needed it. Besides, it was a party. A little glass would be fun. It would, after all, be just the once. Feel the focus again, the engine driving me forward. One time to remember.

And with that final thought, the battle was lost.

It was almost midnight. Upstairs, my girlfriend asked the room if they had seen me while I flopped on another shitty couch in a barely lit room smelling of rot and drugs. Quickly, before I could change my mind, I took a long drag off the pipe and held it in my lungs. As the ball dropped, as my friends cracked party poppers, I got high.

Later, I went back upstairs. I spoke too loud and too fast. I danced and sweat and made manic jokes. In my head - and only in my head - I brought that party back to life.

The next day was the first of 2005. A fresh start. In the middle of the afternoon, after being wide awake for thirty hours, nothing seemed smarter than to visit a house I'd spent months avoiding and buy an eight ball of dope.

Like that, I lost three more years of my life.

For I do not do the good I want to do, but the evil I do not want to do - this I keep on doing. Now if I do what I do not want to do, it is no longer I who do it, but it is sin living in me that does it.   - Romans 7:20-21

Duffel Bag

"You're fucked, man." I was hanging out with Jared, a wiry kid a few years younger than me. We sat, as always, in a room darkened against the midday sun. He took a long hit off the bong and said again, "You are so fucked."

A month into my second run at killing myself with glass, it had already become a grind. A year had passed but there was still no steady dealer, no Dude, no Fin, so every day I scrambled across town searching for poor quality weight at terrible prices. I'd use too much myself then spend the next few days trying to sell the rest. It was miserable, and I knew it was miserable as I experienced it, but I didn't care. I had a new ambition to keep me going: I wanted to climb my way to the top of the trash heap. I was going to be the next Fin.

The competition wasn't fierce. Generally, small towns users have few ambitions outside their next fix.

Occasionally someone would start moving serious weight, but something - the police, their addiction, a rival dealer - would stop them within a few months at most. I had seen it happen again and again. Even Fin, who made it longer than most, eventually came to an ugly end. Still, my meth-coated brain was convinced of its own brilliance. I would be smarter than the others. I'd keep a step ahead of the authorities. I'd be the new Fin, but better: I'd never get caught.

Stoned, Jared giggled into his fist. "You are a wanted man," he said. "They're coming for you."

"What the hell?"

"Your brother pissed off the wrong people. Dre think he stole a duffle bag out of his apartment and they're coming after you unless he returns their shit."

Dre was a former associate of Fin's. He wasn't quite a monster like our old boss, but he had connections to a gang out of Saint Paul. According to Jared some members of this gang were looking to drag me up to the cities and lock me in a basement until my brother gave back their stuff.

I leaned back and closed my eyes. Drug users are notoriously paranoid so I asked, "Did he do it?"

"Does it matter?"

"Nah," I said. "I guess not." I massaged my temples, trying to calm my thoughts. Six weeks ago I had been selling lawn tractors at Sears. "What should I do?"

"Nothing. That's what I'm saying. You're fucked." His laugh turned into a smoker's cough.

I muttered a curse. Jesse had screwed me over. For a rash moment I wanted to find him and rough him up; make it clear he needed to get out of Red Wing and never show his face in my town again. But I swallowed my anger. It wouldn't help the problem and I needed to think.

It didn't take long to go through my options. I hadn't seen my brother in weeks and didn't know where he was. It wasn't in my nature to run and I had no place to hide. I couldn't ignore it; these were serious guys and they'd have little problem killing me. No, as far as I could tell, I had only one move.

I said, "You heard this from Dre?"

"Yeah."

"You know him?

Jared stared up at me, his face a shadow. "I guess."

"Know where he is?"

"I know where he hangs out."

"All right." I stood up. "Let's pay the man a visit."

With a shrug, Jared followed me outside. We squinted into the sun. Across the street a mother was pushing a stroller down the sidewalk. It always surprised me to see normal people going about their lives: buying groceries, driving to work, playing in a park. Aliens, all of them. People like me and Dre and Jared, we lived in a different world.

We climbed into my car and Jared directed me to an old rental a few blocks from downtown. A cracked driveway led to a house with tattered gray siding. A few men leaned against a parked car, smoking. They nodded at us when we passed.

Jared knocked for me. As we waited, the danger of what I was doing, confronting a man who wanted to lock me in a basement, started to penetrate the glass-fueled haze in my brain. I shuffled from foot to foot, the wood spongy underneath me. I clenched and unclenched my fists. I needed to calm down. Be cool. But my heart thumped into my throat.

My eyes flicked around as Jared knocked again. Guy lighting a cigarette. Plastic bag stuck to a branch. A dead animal - large, like a muskrat - laid under a near-by bush. I rested a hand against the railing but didn't trust it with any weight.

The door opened, and a man - a big dude with sleepy eyes - peered out at us. "Hey," he said. "Jared, what's up?"

"Dre here?"

The man nodded. His movements were slow as he stepped back to let us in.

We stood in a cramped living room. Cardboard had been duct-taped over the windows. It was quiet and be-sides the guy who opened the door there didn't seem to be anyone else there. The TV was on, the letters AUX glowed white on the black screen. A couple Xbox controllers sat on the carpet.

The man was staring at us.

Jared said, "Where is he?"

"Who?"

"Dre."

"Oh right. He's…" The guy pointed vaguely towards the back of the house.

"Could you find him?"

"Sure."

"Thanks."

The guy picked at his shirt sleeve.

"Could you get him now?"

He looked at Jared as if he were piecing together a puzzle. "Yeah," he said. And after a slow first step he drifted down the hallway.

Jared filled the silence as we waited with a low patter of nonsense. He shifted his weight, rubbed his hands together, and scratched above his ear. Glass made it impossible for most people to stand still, but I had calmed down. My panic had been soothed by dope into something more like excitement.

I felt like I was entering a high stakes poker game when Dre appeared through a door. He was smaller than Fin and not nearly as smart or dangerous, but he wanted to be. He had a wide face, hard with anger, but it lacked menace. He rubbed at his eyes like he had just woken up.

"What's this?"

"Dre," Jared said, "you know Ben."

He opened his mouth wide, startled. Then he caught himself. "Jesse's brother."

"Yeah."

He lowered his head but raised his eyes to glare at me. "He's got my shit."

I shrugged. "I don't know anything about that."

His body tensed. Part of me wanted to back away but I breathed that down and stood still. He said, "Brother stole from me."

I didn't try staring him down, but just shook my head. "I've got nothing to do with it. He and I, we're disconnected."

"This why you here?"

"Yeah, it's why I'm here. Just... don't confuse my brother and me."

He grunted. Tilted his head. Bugged out his eyes. I kept my face calm and tried not to look away.

"All right," he said, and everything relaxed. He lowered his shoulders and scratched his chest. "That's cool." He flopped onto the couch, dug a bag of dope out of his pocket, and it was over.

Adrenaline pumped in my body - and it had no place to go. It had been too easy; I was revved up, ready for a fight but Jared was settling in for a smoke. Dre prepared a bong and passed it to Jared. Jared took a hit and passed it back. I stood, feeling out of place, unsure what to do.

"So," I said. "We're cool."

Dre leaned forward to turn on the Xbox. "We're cool," he said. "But tell your brother - I want my shit back."

I left the house and walked down the sidewalk on high alert. A quiet evening, I could hear my shoes scratch against the concrete. At the street, both the men and the car were gone. No suspicious vehicles were parked nearby. No strange noises. Safe in my car, I figured that was it. If they were going to grab me they would have done it.

I had faced the man. I solved the problem. Unused adrenaline mixed with speed and I screamed out into the night as I drove. I was a hustler, a gangster, an unstoppable force. I'd own this town.

For days I celebrated my victory as I went about my

business; hustling up drugs, using too much and selling the leftovers for profit. Then, one afternoon less than a week after I confronted Dre, my phone rang. I stared at the display, trying to decide whether I should answer. He'd need something, probably a ride. It wouldn't be the first time I ignored one of his calls. Still, he was family.

"Hey Ben, shit. Listen. She stranded…" the phone crackled and went silent.

"Jesse?"

"…pick me up?"

His voice had an edge, like he was about to call me a dumbass, like he was doing me a favor by calling. A tone which said he was still the big brother and I better not forget it. Anger rumbled up hot from my gut.

"Ben? You there?"

"Yeah."

He named a gas station in Ellsworth - a little town in Wisconsin - and hung up. I resisted throwing the phone against the wall and instead drove out to get him.

Fifteen minutes later I pulled up to the sidewalk. He squatted on the curb, smoking a cigarette; his clothes wrinkled and unwashed. A cold sore blistered his bottom lip.

He didn't greet me when he sat in my car, but said he needed to go to a house near Red Wing. It was one of those places tweakers gathered to get high. A mother and a son about my age owned it and would often smoke together. Even as messed up as I was, this seemed particularly twisted; but it never stopped me from visiting.

"Hey asshole," I said. We had barely pulled out of the parking lot. "What the hell?"

"What?"

"You set Dre after me."

"Oh yeah, shit, sorry about that."

"What the hell?"

"He thinks I stole some bag of his."

"Did you?"

"Nah."

"Bullshit."

"No bullshit. It wasn't me," he said. "I heard it was just a few clothes and a little dope. What's the big deal?"

"That was it?"

"And maybe a little cash." He scratched at something on the back of his head. "Is what I heard."

"They were coming after me to get it back."

"Yeah." Jesse laughed and I wanted to punch him in the throat. "Yeah, I heard about that."

"You got to take care of this."

"I can't give the man back what I don't have."

I told him how I met with Dre, how I looked him in the eye and talked with him man to man.

"That worked?"

I shrugged. "I'm here talking to you."

We rumbled across the Mississippi on an old metal bridge.

"All right. Shit." Jesse rolled down his window; stared blankly at the downtown storefronts. "I'll talk to him."

"When?"

"When I get to it."

"How about you get to it now?"

His eyes widened, and I saw a little shiver of fear. But I felt no pity.

"You serious?"

I turned towards Dre's house at the next intersection.

His shoulders slumped. "Ah shit," he said.

It was late afternoon, almost dusk, and the heat of the day had given way to a comfortable evening breeze. I pulled in front of the house, my right tire pushing up against the curb. Dre sat on the front step, smoking with two others. None of them looked up.

"This is a bad idea."

"You got no choice, Jess." I lowered my voice to a growl. "This, or leave town. For good."

He stared at me. I had surprised myself but there was no going back. I didn't want to be anyone's little brother any more.

"A bad idea," he said. He swore under his breath first but he climbed out. When he shut his door, the eyes of the three men darted in our direction. Dre had been laughing but fell silent when he saw Jesse. His eyes turned hard.

Jesse raised both hands as he approached. I watched from the car. His voice came as a murmur through the windshield.

There was laughter and a group of boys streaked past me on their bikes - small town kids, oblivious. I watched them until they turned the corner.

When I looked back Dre was moving. He had gripped something sharp and metal, a bolt maybe, and swung it down against my brother's face. Three hard blows and Jesse sank to a knee. Then three more and he fell to his side. He curled up, knees to his chest, and buried his head in his arms.

I stayed where I was. Not because of fear; I could handle myself in a fistfight. No, I watched that man kick the shit out of my brother out of ambition, a toxic need to get ahead. After almost four years of addiction, my capacity for empathy had been replaced with hunger. I needed Dre. He was respected. He had access to a better quality product. His connections would expand my operation. So I shoved down any leftover emotions I had for my big brother by thinking, "It's not my fight." And, "He's got it coming."

After a last punch, Dre stepped back and wiped his hand against the back of his pants. He said something I couldn't hear, and gave a hard kick to Jesse's back. He shouted, "Get the fuck out of here," but my brother didn't move. Still I hung back, but as the seconds passed I realized I was holding my breath. Dre shook his head and said something to the others. He lit a cigarette as they laughed.

Finally, a flicker of movement. Jesse straightened one of his legs, uncurled his body and slowly sat up. Blood smeared down his cheek and soaked into his collar. No one helped him as he stood or as he staggered back towards the car. He slumped in next to me and neither of us said a word as I pulled away.

After turning at the corner, Dre's house out of sight, I asked, "Where to?"

Jesse couldn't open his right eye. Purple bruises were already swelling on his cheek. He needed a doctor, but said, "Jamie."

"What's that?"

"Girl I'm with." He named a street on the far side of town.

We drove in silence until I saw lights in my mirror: a police car. I spit out a string of curse words. I had some glass in my pocket, just a little for personal use - and I assumed Jesse was carrying too. It wouldn't be enough for prison, I didn't think, but it was enough to screw up my plans. Enough to get a criminal record, enough to be a known target for the police.

"Just be cool," Jesse said.

I didn't answer, but silently I screamed at him. This was his fault. He must have a warrant out, or some neighbor called when they spotted him bleeding in Dre's front lawn. If I was going down, it was because of him.

The officer stood at the window; he was shorter, with a thick neck and a closely shaved head. He said, "You know you got a headlight out?"

"I do?"

"Yeah." He shined his flashlight at Jesse. "What happened to you?"

My brother was quiet for a moment. He rubbed his hand a few times on his knee. Then he said, "I fell."

"Is that right?"

"Yeah," he said.

"Hell of a fall."

"I was skateboarding."

He peered at us both and flicked the flashlight around the car. "Skateboarding," he said, then grinned at the obvious lie. "All right - get going." He shook his head.

"Get yourself to the doctor. And fix your headlight." He tapped the roof of my car and waved us on.

I pulled away from the curb. We hadn't been arrested but I was still furious. In the short drive to the girl's house I wanted to scream at him, maybe get in a few blows of my own, but we didn't speak. Finally, he left my car without a word.

A couple days later I reached out to Dre. The whole situation had been a mess, but as I was focused singularly on getting ahead, I searched for an angle, a way to work it for my advantage. I showed Dre respect and shared some weight. I claimed credit for getting my brother to show up. He appreciated it, and in turn introduced me up the chain. Through him, I was able to connect with a better supplier.

The next time I saw my brother his eye was still swollen and he walked with a limp - but we didn't speak to each other or even make eye contact. Something had broken between us which hasn't fully healed to this day. But I didn't care about that. I had moved up. My network had grown. In my glass-twisted brain, I counted the experience as a win.

For whoever wants to save their life will lose it, but whoever loses their life for me will save it. What good is it for someone to gain the whole world, and yet lose or forfeit their very self? - Luke 9:24-25

Ambush

Derek leaned back against the couch. "I heard some dude's up in River Falls messing in your territory," he said.

This was news to me. "Who'd you hear that from?"

"It's going around."

"Yeah, but who told you?"

He thought for a second. "I don't remember."

"Huh." I took another hit. No idea what time it was, but it was late. Derek and I sat together in a house everyone in our world knew. It was in a nice neighborhood. Outside dads would toss baseballs to their kids as moms chatted with each other on the sidewalk, but inside, at night, tweakers gathered to get high.

Derek pointed a finger at me, "I could look into it for you," he said, "if you want."

I stared at him; blinked a few times. After the situation with Dre, I had moved up. I was a long way from being the man like Fin, but I had access to a better product, my margins improved and my customer base expanded. With a little cash in my pocket, I started acting like I was in the movie Goodfellas. I had watched it a dozen times, but only paid attention to the good parts: Henry Hill taking a date to the club, walking behind the scenes, tipping everyone he passed, getting a table that didn't exist for regular schnooks. Since I was still too young to legally drink or go clubbing, I'd peel twenties off a giant roll of cash to pay for a bag of Cheetos at a gas station. At the bakery I'd leave a ten dollar tip for a jelly donut.

Along with all this, I had a group of guys start hanging with me. They were users and I had the weight so they wanted to be my best friend. They'd look for me in a room and make sure to sit close. They'd lean in and listen when I talked.

Derek had become one of these guys. He showed up a couple weeks before and offered to get me a beer. After that, I'd see him every couple of days. My childhood bully laughed at my jokes and asked me every few minutes if I needed anything; honestly, it was pretty great.

This, however - roughing up the competition - was something new.

"Look into it for me?" I said.

"I'll make a few calls, see what's up. If there's a problem I'll get some guys and take care of it."

He was offering to be the muscle. The guy who threw lit matches at me, who stole a pistol when he was thirteen, who scared the piss out of me for twenty years; he wanted to help me out by working security and collect when people refused to pay. In return he'd get a good deal on dope and some free stuff here and there. It was how the game worked.

I tried to look tough but couldn't help grinning; I had taken one step closer to being like Fin - and through Derek of all people. "Yeah, check that out for me," I said. "Let me know what's up."

He nodded seriously and took off. When I saw him a couple days later, he told me it was legit. A dealer was pushing into my territory two towns away.

He asked, "What do you want to do about it?"

Petty dealers worked in every small town. This guy was probably selling without thinking and was not a real threat. The smart choice would be to let it go, but I had Derek standing near, looking eager to work with me. And it was part of the fantasy. Henry Hill wouldn't allow it, neither would Fin.

I suppressed the grin this time and said, "Let's pay the man a visit."

Derek and I took two others, both users willing to do it for a little glass, and we drove up the river about forty-five minutes into Wisconsin. A little after midnight one of my customers called this dealer over to his place. Meanwhile, we snuck between the buildings in his apartment complex. Keeping a view of the parking lot, we hid in the shadows. I crouched behind a bush. When he showed up, we'd be ready.

It was a cold night in late October and fifteen minutes in I started freezing my ass off. I knelt in damp dirt which soaked through my jeans. Every time I moved - because my leg fell asleep or I spotted headlights on the road - branches scratched into my face. Each minute this guy didn't show I felt more ridiculous.

After a solid half hour, I finally stood and pushed my way out of the bushes. Back under the light of the street lamp I called to the others like I was ending a game of hide and seek.

On the drive home, the drugs kept us safe from embarrassment. Instead of feeling like idiots waiting for a dealer smart enough not to show - we bragged about what we would do to the guy if given the chance.

Outside my house, after the others had gone home, I had a rare moment of reflection. My car idled in the driveway and I thought through what I had been doing. Because of several of fortunate accidents, I had never assaulted anyone for my business. And because of working with Fin, I had rules. Some were his, some I made up for myself. I'd threaten but never hurt. I wouldn't sell to minors. I wouldn't cut my product with dangerous chemicals. I wouldn't sell to someone just out of treatment. I was a drug dealer, I knew, but I twisted it around so I was one of the good guys. Or if not good, exactly, I wasn't a monster.

My conscience was clear. I shut off the car and went to bed. Because of an accident - a guy didn't show up and give me the opportunity to beat the hell out of him - I was doing okay. I was doing better than okay: a bully from my childhood, Derek, had become one of my associates. I was on exactly the right path, doing what needed to be done. I was winning. That night, high on glass, I believed my own bullshit and went to bed in peace.

Meanwhile on the other side of town a man on meth threw his two-year old daughter down a stairwell in the panic of a police raid. I didn't personally sell to this guy but I was a part of the same world. I was actively poisoning my community. Looking back on it almost a decade later, it still keeps me up at night. I can't stop thinking of what I did: I helped people kill themselves with drugs.

Create in me a clean heart, O God,
  and put a new and right spirit within me.
                                         - Psalm 51:10

The Legend

Dark room. Ratty couch. Several people, men and women, sitting around getting high. Same as every day, but there was a new face in the corner; he looked familiar but I couldn't place him. Three guys sat near him and I could tell by the way they leaned in, the way their eyes kept searching his face for cues: he was a man with serious weight.

I studied him as I smoked. Everything in my life had been reduced to the hustle. The supplier I found through Dre was all right, but he charged too much for a product cut with powder. I was ready to move around him. Derek rambled next to me, telling a story I only half listened to. When he stopped for breath, I said, "Who is that dude?"

"The little guy? That's Chase."

"Chase?" A memory stirred from my childhood. "What's his deal?"

"Shit, you don't remember? He grew up around here - he rode my bus for a year or two. Dude's a legend."

I half remembered. Chase was older than me and went to prison soon after he turned eighteen for dealing drugs. According to Derek he had only recently been released - and almost immediately showed up in Red Wing with a heavy supply of high quality glass.

Derek continued to ramble but I stopped listening and leaned back into the couch. Through slit eyes, I studied Chase, my mind hammering at the problem. The man had something I needed: a better source with a better deal.

I didn't even introduce myself that first afternoon. Instead, I spent the next few weeks learning what I could about him. No one knew much, but I found out he hooked up with a top-level supplier through prison contacts. This information drove me nuts. It seemed perversely unfair that I was at a disadvantage for having never been arrested.

I fell into a sulk. Everything was screwed up. I'd never get ahead. Something always went wrong. Someone didn't pay right when I needed the money. Or my car broke down on the way to a buy. Or the seller cut the product to shit and didn't tell me. There was always something, a force pushing against me, making my life an uphill slog.

Looking back, there was some truth to this. I did feel a presence pushing against me, slowing me down. Was it karma? Bad luck? Drug dealing is a contract with the devil, so was it an evil force? A demon? On the other hand, the more things went wrong, the less drugs

I could sell. Strange accidents kept me from doing violence to others. Maybe it was God. Perhaps an angel protected me from the worst parts of myself.

Angel, demon or chance, I didn't know but it pissed me off. I needed to get through Chase to his supplier. He was nothing more than another obstacle in my way - and one I could handle. He was the opposite of Fin: smaller, thin, soft-spoken. He commanded neither fear nor respect. And I was far from the naive kid I had been when I started. Experience and heavy drug use had hardened me.

A January afternoon, six weeks later; Thanksgiving and Christmas had passed without my noticing. I sat in another broken chair in another musty room with blankets tacked over the windows. Chase came in alone, bringing an icy breeze through the front door. He sat in the corner and prepared a pipe.

I introduced myself. Making conversation was easy for me - whether with gangbangers, toothless old men or rising drug lords. I mentioned Diamond Bluff. Told him he was a legend. He lit up. Tweakers as a rule are always happy to talk and he was no exception. We compared people we both knew, searching for overlap. He didn't remember my brother, but he had heard of Derek. Then he offered me his pipe.

I took a hit. It was high quality, exactly the kind of stuff I needed to be selling. But I swallowed my frustration and said, "This is good shit."

He smiled. Glass didn't rot my teeth; I'm not sure why, but Chase hadn't been so lucky. He said, "It's the best."

"I believe it." I was relaxed. Breezy. Just making friendly conversation. "Mexico?"

He arched an eyebrow. All the glass of any quality came from Mexico. But he said, "I know some guys; they get me a deal. If you need some, let me know."

"Thanks. This is potent stuff." I tried to keep my voice casual. "How often do you get up there?"

"Whenever you want."

"Yeah? Like every day or what?"

"Nah." It was a stupid question but he didn't seem to mind. "Like once a week. But I get enough."

"Well it's good shit."

"I got a kid runs up there for me." He nodded across the room to a kid who looked about the age I had been when I started. I'd seen him around. His name was Dylan.

"Cool," I said. Chase kept talking but I stopped listening. Instead, I made eye contact with Dylan and nodded a greeting.

Soon, I thought, I'd have to sit down and have a friendly talk with that kid about his future.

The acquisition of treasures by a lying tongue
Is a fleeting vapor, the pursuit of death.
*   - Proverbs 21:6*

Storm Shelter

The highway blurred in front of us. I drove, eyes wide, jittery with excitement. My tolerance to glass was such that I didn't fidget anymore, but the thrill of the moment made it hard to keep still. Dylan and I were on our way to meet his contact, Chase's current supplier - soon to be mine.

It had been so easy. A week after my conversation with Chase I had met with Dylan. We smoked up together - my glass, my bong. I shrugged off his thanks. I had spent days considering my approach and decided to be straight with him.

"How's working with Chase?"

He held up a hand. Took a hit. Exhaled. "It's all right."

"He compensate you fairly?"

He grinned. "It's all right."

"Yeah?"

He shrugged.

I said, "If an opportunity came up to..."

"I'd take it."

I startled at his answer - then tried to hide it with a laugh. I had expected a challenge, some resistance, a series of conversations and negotiations. But he had accepted my offer before I made it. We quickly settled on a price and Dylan no longer worked for Chase. And Chase wasn't the kind of guy to come after you. Unlike Fin he'd let this slide.

It was that easy.

From there, Dylan made contact with Chase's supplier in Minneapolis and arranged for us to meet. And now, a week later, it was time for the first buy.

A huge day. After this I would shoot ahead of the competition. I tapped the steering wheel. I bounced with the music. I tried to play it cool for Dylan but this was too big. I had everything. It had all worked out, thank God.

Thank God? A sour note. Where did that come from? What I was doing was the farthest thing from God. The thought nagged at me, but I tried to shake it off as we approached the house.

Dylan directed me to park and we stepped out of the car. Noise from a major highway pounded from less than a block away. Lawns were unmowed. Wooded fences rotted and bowed in towards the ground. Next door the windows were boarded up, but we stepped up to a house with a sturdy porch - and a working light - and knocked on its freshly painted door.

It was happening. I was about to get everything I had wanted. Except... the earlier thought of God brought unwanted memories: Father Thomas - my childhood priest. The smell of incense. The way chanting echoed around the church. The body of Christ, given for me.

A terrible thought came into my head: I should run. I needed to get off this porch, get back in my car and leave this business behind.

But that was crazy. And it made no sense - I was winning. This was everything I wanted. I rubbed hard at the back of my neck; I needed to get my mind right. I was here. I was all in. I was about to get rich.

The door opened. Inside the light was dim, and the air smoky. In a narrow living room two guys lounged on a couch while two girls leaned over them. Three were smoking cigarettes, one smoked dope. The scene helped me shove away the sour memories of church. I had a roll of fifty hundred dollar bills in my pocket and these were serious people.

The guy who opened the door peered at me. A thin man, his eyes were dark under his baseball cap. He asked me some questions - who I knew, what happened with Chase. I had people who vouched for me, but I was still a skinny twenty-one year old kid with bleach-blonde hair.

Finally, he said, "Got my money?"

Apparently my answers had satisfied him. I dug in my pocket and gave him the cash. He ruffled through it, looking bored.

"All right. Follow me."

He took me down a back stairway into a basement which was little more than a storm shelter. Crumbling brick walls held up a low ceiling. Water stains covered the concrete floor. I had to duck under a wooden arch to step into the main room.

A hanging lightbulb swayed between us as he opened a safe and brought out the biggest ziplock bag I had ever seen. It bulged with pure glass: giant crystals, several pounds worth. The man held a million dollars easy in his hands.

He grabbed a clear plastic cup, the kind you'd use for water at a fast food restaurant, and started scooping crystals into a second, smaller bag. Clearly this one was meant for me. Two scoops covered what I had paid for, but he didn't stop. He kept going back, dumping more - and within seconds I owed them the kind of cash that would get a man killed.

The world began to spin like I stood up too fast. My thinking grew mushy and I couldn't quite figure out how I had gotten there. I had a great childhood. After-noons I'd throw rocks into the river. Evenings I'd sit by a campfire. Weekends I'd hunt with my dad. Nights I'd sit near my mom and watch TV. My cousin and I had spent days biking around Red Wing or playing street hockey. It was normal as far as that went. My parents were good people. They worked hard. They brought me to church.

But there I was in a Minneapolis basement being fronted an impossible amount of drugs by a man who'd murder me with a shrug. I thought I had wanted this but it was all wrong. Something had happened to me and I got all twisted up. I pumped my system full of poison until my goals became perverse: Climb to the top. Scramble for as much as I could - money, drugs, power - and forget everything else.

I lost my family. I lost my friends. I lost my faith.

I was about to become just like Fin, something I had worked towards for years. I should have been happy, triumphant, but standing in that basement, all of my illusions began to collapse around me. Everything was a lie. I wasn't a good-natured outlaw smuggling moonshine. This was no game. No, these guys were monsters - and I was too.

The man handed me the bag and told me when they expected payment. He didn't have to say it, but they'd kill me if I didn't deliver. This, however, didn't bother me. I knew every user within 50 miles of my house. Soon, I'd get them their cash and return for more.

But I had had a moment of terrible clarity and I wanted to get away as fast as I could. I shoved the glass into a backpack and hurried with Dylan back to my car. It was a struggle not to speed all the way back to Red Wing.

I had felt the presence of death in that house. And no matter how fast I moved I'd never outrun it.

The fool says in his heart,
   "There is no God."
They are corrupt, and their ways are vile;
   there is no one who does good.
God looks down from heaven
   on all mankind
to see if there are any who understand,
   any who seek God.

                    - Psalm 53:1-2

S for Schmidt

"Where's my truck?"

"I don't know, Ben, that's what I'm trying to tell you."

"Jared."

"I don't know."

"Where the hell's my truck?"

"I told you. I left it for a couple seconds and it was gone."

I swore at him and hung up. Things were going well. My deal with the Minneapolis house was working out better than I hoped. That truck was one of the first nice things I owned. After the truck I had bought a Hummer. Even factoring in my own massive use, I was bringing in real cash - enough to shut down my conscience for awhile.

Jared, the guy who introduced me to Dre, started hanging around now along with a few others, associates who were just like me when I worked with Fin. Once I had the weight, they became my best friends. They'd do me favors, just about anything I asked, and in return I'd front them some product, give them discounts, and only one stupid time, loan them my truck.

I called Derek. He had become about as trusted an associate as I ever had in that world and knew some of the right people. After we talked, he called a couple guys in Saint Paul and asked them to watch for my truck.

It took less than 24 hours. His friends had asked around and the next day Derek called me with an exact location of my missing truck. We met up a few minutes later and drove the Hummer up to retrieve it.

An hour later, we pulled down a street in Saint Paul, not far from the house where I met Roach and the Butcher, and spotted my truck, a tan Ford F150 with two chrome Superman stickers on the back. In my mind, the 'S' stood for Schmidt.

It was a beautiful day, warm and sunny, and the street was filled with people, kids chasing each other down the sidewalk, men and women standing around smoking and laughing.

Derek and I planned our approach as we took a wide loop around the neighborhood. It was a thin strand that kept me connected to my humanity, but I felt uncomfortable causing a scene in front of kids, particularly if it could turn violent. We hadn't brought any firearms with us, but we didn't know what the truck thieves would do.

Still, like always, I favored the direct approach. So

the next time we swung around the block, we turned down the street and parked a few houses down from my truck. From the Hummer, I peered through the truck's back window. Through the glare I could see the shadow of a large person in the driver's seat.

I grabbed a pair of mechanics' gloves from the back seat, figuring I might have to fight. I didn't want to get some drug user's blood on my hands. The idea was to leave with my truck, not hepatitis.

Across the street a young woman must have seen me pull on these gloves, and got the wrong idea, because as soon as I opened the door she yelled, "He's got a gun!"

People screamed. Everyone scattered. Doors slammed shut. I raised my empty hands but no one stopped to look. The street deserted in seconds.

I smirked at Derek. Once again, everything seemed to tumble my way. I pushed aside any thoughts of God and thanksgiving before they could become a problem and hurried to the truck.

A heavyset woman with wide, wet eyes was sitting in the driver's seat. She batted her hands and screamed out a long string of colorful curses. She didn't seem to be a threat but I grabbed her by the elbow. She moved willingly, she knew it had been stolen, but she swore the entire way, putting words in combinations so disgusting it almost shocked me.

The woman disappeared into a house and I reclaimed my truck. After a quick search I found the keys were in the ignition and the only thing missing was a pair of speakers.

I pulled away - Derek followed behind in the Hummer - and I knew I had made it. I had become so well connected I found my stolen property in less than a day, quicker than any cop could. I beat a rhythm against the steering wheel with a goofy smile on my face. All that nagging shit about God and death, my old church, my childhood priest, I successfully smothered it with power and money. I had Derek working for me. I had two expensive vehicles and a house. I had become the new Fin.

And like those S stickers in the back of my truck, for a while I thought it was cool.

Jesus said, "For judgment I have come into this world, so that the blind will see and those who see will become blind." *- John 9:39*

Early 2008

The Lord is my shepherd; I shall not want. He makes me to lie down in green pastures; He leads me beside the still waters. He restores my soul; He leads me in the paths of righteousness for His name's sake. Yea, though I walk through the valley of the shadow of death, I will fear no evil; For You are with me; Your rod and Your staff, they comfort me. You prepare a table before me in the presence of my enemies; You anoint my head with oil; My cup runs over. Surely goodness and mercy shall follow me all the days of my life; And I will dwell in the house of the Lord. Forever. The Lord is my shepherd; I shall not want. He makes me to lie down in green pastures; He leads me beside the still waters. He restores my soul; He leads me in the paths of righteousness for His name's sake. Yea, though I walk through the valley of the shadow of death, I will fear no evil; For You are with me; Your rod and Your staff, they comfort me. You prepare a table before me in the presence of my enemies; You anoint my head with oil; My cup runs over. Surely

The Slap

Healthy people smiled around me with round faces and bright eyes. Some were drunk but for the most part they talked about normal human things in normal tones of voice. A regular party for real people, an old high school friend had invited me. It was late afternoon and he was grilling hot dogs.

I wore my cap low so it cast a shadow across my eyes and a jacket too warm for the weather. In a back pocket I had a little packet of glass which felt like a secret - a hidden identity. I was a mole, sent up to spy from the underworld, walking around the healthy as if I were one of them.

Someone handed me a beer - I had recently turned 21 - and I sipped at it while taking in the scene. I felt someone staring at me, and I swiveled my head, searching for the source until my eyes met Alyssa's. She was perched on a wood stump by the fire. I hadn't seen her or her brother Micah in more than a year. I smiled as best I could but my gut tightened like it was about to get punched. The ground grew unsteady underneath me. Back at home, in a basement safe I had enough drugs to light up the entire party for a week. A second earlier this secret life had made me feel special, but it now felt hollow. I barely saw my family. I hadn't seen my sister in months. She was doing okay, I thought, but I didn't know, not really.

Alyssa didn't smile back. I tried to shrug it off, told myself she probably hadn't seen me, but I needed a moment to clear my head. I stepped through the screen door and down the hallway towards the bathroom.

I splashed cold water on my face and carefully avoided looking at the mirror. I took a few deep breaths. I reached back and touched the packet of drugs I had in my back pocket. I didn't need to feel this way. It had been a mistake to come. It was time to leave.

When I came out, Alyssa was standing in the hallway.

I smiled again but her eyes were hard.

"Is it true?

"Hey Alyssa. Long time."

She shook her head. "Is it true?"

"What do you mean?"

"About the meth. Is it true?"

Of course it was true, but I didn't want to tell her that, so I shrugged.

She slapped me hard across the face. The sting made my eyes water.

"Stop it!" she screamed at me. She clenched her fist,

then pointed a finger at my chest. "It's not cool. It's not fun. It's going to kill you."

"Whoa!" I raised my hands up in surrender.

"Asshole!"

"I'm sorry," I said.

"I don't give a shit if you're sorry, Ben. Stop it."

I opened my mouth - to say what I don't know - but she spun away from me and walked off. My cheek was warm where I touched my hand to it. A few minutes later I snuck out the front door without saying good bye. I didn't belong in that world and it had been a mistake to go. Twenty minutes later I was in a basement, doing what I had to do in order to forget.

"Whoever walks in the dark does not know where they are going. Believe in the light while you have the light, so that you may become children of light."

- John 12:35b-36

Jeeps

They were watching me, the cops and gangs both. Or I thought they were; my drug habit had intensified and it was hard to tell the difference between paranoia and reality. But I had to keep my shit together. And I had to keep things moving; without constant motion it would all collapse. I had some of the same responsibilities as anyone: I had a mortgage. My girlfriend and I had gotten married so I even had a wife. I needed to act normal.

I kept everything nice. I washed and waxed my vehicles. In the fall I sprayed leaves off my driveway. I walked out in the evening and got my mail. In the winter I got high and snow-blowed every driveway on my street.

Middle of the afternoon one spring day I went out to mow my lawn. As I reached the end of a row and turned the mower around, a jeep drove by my house. I watched it until it turned down a side street. It was no big deal; we lived on a busy road and it was just a Jeep. Or was there a guy in the back seat? I searched for it between the houses, letting the mower idle on the grass. Another car passed, and finally I blinked. I had been standing still for several minutes. I shook my head. My brain was fuzzy. I started down a new row but had to stop when a Jeep passed, different than the first. An older model but the same dark color. The driver turned to stare at me; he was wearing dark glasses and a dark suit. Or was he? As it drifted around a curve, I couldn't quite picture it. Was he wearing a suit? Why would he be wearing a suit?

I had to keep moving. People were staring. My elderly neighbor was watching me through his garage as I stood stupidly, mower running, gazing at the street.

Another fucking jeep went by. This one had someone in the back seat, face up against the glass. Or I thought it did. It was darkly tinted and I wasn't looking directly at it but through the edge of my vision I saw something. Eyes. Staring at me.

I worried over my wife. Where was she? She was safe. She was in the house. Where was my weight? I had a lot in my basement. Should I flush it? I figured I should flush it.

I blinked and I was still standing there. People were staring. Another Jeep drove by. Or that last one might not have been a Jeep. I couldn't tell but it was all messed up. And I needed to finish mowing the lawn. They were watching. I couldn't leave it half-mowed. That'd be something a lunatic would do. It'd be something a crazed drug dealer would do.

I stashed the mower in the garage and counted in my head as the door closed behind me. How many Jeeps had passed? I couldn't remember. Was it the same Jeep doing circles? No, I was sure it wasn't. But a fleet of Jeeps maybe, following me. Watching me.

Where was the weight? I couldn't remember and slapped the palm of my hand against the side of my head. No, I was being stupid. The drugs were in the basement, locked in the safe. I was freaking out and needed to stop. I was fine. No problem. It was all fine.

Someone pounded their fist against the garage door. I froze up. They had come for me. Tears welled in my eyes, and I rubbed at them hard, thinking about my mother. She had been the best. She raised me right - and not for this life. She didn't deserve to watch one of her boys waste away in prison.

Another knock. Would the police knock? Something about that didn't make sense.

"Ben!" A familiar voice from the other side. "It's Dylan."

A flood of relief. I said a semi-prayer of thanksgiving. The whole time I had been praying without meaning to, whispering a cry for help to anyone who would listen.

Dylan closed the door behind him. Another dim garage, another face in shadows. He was talking, but I couldn't follow. His words were mushy and slow.

I was moving. I didn't want to but I couldn't stay still. The cops were outside and I was fucked. I didn't understand why Dylan was so calm - and where was my wife?

Eight hundred bucks. I understood those words. He owed me money. He needed to pay up, but didn't have the cash. He wasn't giving me the cash. Rage twisted inside me and I was screaming. I don't remember starting to scream but Dylan was on the ground, his head turned away and I had a weapon in my hand; I couldn't breathe the anger squeezed my chest and words spit from my mouth.

He started to cry, this kid. Begging me. And I couldn't look at him so I turned away and screamed at him to get out of my garage. He scrambled off and left me alone. In the dark.

I felt the presence pushing against me, the one that lived in shadows. It squeezed my chest and sank down my throat. I gagged but didn't fight. It owned me. I belonged to the darkness.

Outside a car rumbled down the street, and I knew from the rattle of the engine that it must be a Jeep.

Now we know that whatever the law says, it says to those who are under the law, so that every mouth may be silenced and the whole world held accountable to God.   *- Romans 3:19*

That's No Cop

"I'm going to kill him. I'm going to mess him up." I was too pissed to care about the order of things. "He's a dead piece of shit."

It was just two of us in my garage: me and Derek. He asked, "Who is?"

"He was saying shit about my wife."

"Who?"

"You don't hate on a man's wife like that."

"You need to calm down, bro."

Derek's soothing voice made me more angry. "I'm going to shoot him in the neck."

"I hear you but…"

"Watch him bleed out."

"Come on, Schmidty."

"You with me?" I stopped pacing and pointed to the door. "Right now. We need to find that asshole."

"Hold up! Who the hell are you talking about?"

I stared at the shadowy space where I knew his face should be. My mouth open and closed. My brain was fuzzy. Someone had disrespected me, I knew it. He said some bad things about my wife. His name and face were there whispering around my head but I couldn't quite catch them. I tried to concentrate but kept coming up blank. Still, my heart raced and my fists clenched the air. I wanted to crush someone's head under my boot.

Derek said, "Let's get out of here. Go do something."

I blinked at him.

"Hey, I got a new pistol back at my house. Let's go shoot."

I shook my head to clear it. Shooting a new pistol did sound like fun. Even this late at night we could park along a quiet stretch of dirt road, fire off a few rounds and no one would notice or care. The idea calmed me and I eyed Derek uncertainly. How had this guy become the voice of reason? Something was wrong. Still, I followed him out to his car.

We crossed into Wisconsin. He lived about fifteen miles from the river near Ellsworth. We moved at a quick clip through the long stretch of farm land. The highway calmed me further. Violence still simmered in my gut, but it lost its urgency. I had to get payback for… I couldn't quite remember what, but it would wait for another day.

We were close to town when headlights appeared in my side mirror. I twisted around to get a better look.

"You got a cop behind you," I said.

He slowed for the town's single stop light and peered into the mirror. "That's not a cop."

I had spent my entire adult life watching behind me for police cars. I said, "I'm telling you it is."

He was driving a red Cadillac with rims, it was well after midnight and he had a warrant out for his arrest. All reasons for caution. But when the light turned green he peeled off, speeding through downtown. He hit fifty a block later as he passed the Dairy Queen. I laughed because to hell with cops and the speed limit. This was the Derek I knew - batshit crazy and reckless.

A quarter mile later the police car turned on its lights.

Derek slammed his fist against the side window and screamed a long series of curses - but he immediately braked, then pulled carefully into a parking lot. He was lit up and pissed, but not enough to try out-driving a cop. He didn't want a felony on top of his drug charges.

The officer stopped behind us; flashing lights cut into our car. Derek shifted, leaning back in his seat so he could dig his hand into his front pocket and pull out a bag of dope. He had a good amount of glass on him - about a gram and a half, a couple hundred dollars worth; as much as a typical user would take in a week, maybe two. He was carrying enough for prison time.

The cop climbed from the car. Derek stuffed the dope into some rolling papers. The cop walked towards us, his shadow tracing his movement along the back window. Derek shoved the papers in his mouth. The cop knocked as Derek took several painful gulps.

I ground my teeth as the officer ordered us from the car. Faceless anger made me jittery and the night was crap all the way through. The more I thought, the more it seemed nothing went right for me, ever. We were just two dudes going to have some harmless fun, but they sat me on a concrete curb and shoved Derek in the back of the police car.

Another cop arrived and together they searched through the Cadillac. Ten minutes had passed since Derek ate his stash. They ripped out his CD player and then his speakers, checking the numbers against a database to see if they were stolen. Fifteen minutes passed. They dug through the back seat. Twenty minutes. They opened his trunk and Derek started to bark.

Months later I asked what he remembered and he could only shrug. In the back of that cop car he twisted and screamed, howling at the ceiling like a wolf then slamming his head against the window with a sickening thump. His eyes swirled around his head. His mind sizzled in glass; he was gone.

There was nothing to be done. I lowered my head and tried to tune him out as I waited. A breeze touched my face and the concrete had turned cold. I shivered. Dawn was hours away. The madman raving in the back seat had been a voice of reason less than an hour before - but that thought was too hard. It freaked me out to see him like this, and what it meant for my own thin grip on reality. I needed to clear my head, follow a different line of thinking. I sat behind Derek's car, outside the reach of the streetlights. I sank into the darkness and let it fill me up. I breathed in the shadow until my friend's cries drifted away.

The cops told me I was free to go. I stood and stretched my back as they drove off. I tried not to watch

Derek howling and thrashing in the back seat. Instead, I gave thanks to the shadow that it hadn't happened to me.

This is the evil in everything that happens under the sun: The same destiny overtakes all. The hearts of people, moreover, are full of evil and there is madness in their hearts while they live, and afterward they join the dead. Anyone who is among the living has hope—even a live dog is better off than a dead lion!

- Ecclesiastes 9:3-4

Security

It grew increasingly difficult to separate real threats from paranoia, so I became more vigilant. I installed security cameras inside and outside my house. Whenever I left I drove around the block several times to study the parked cars. I watched my rear view mirrors and took twisted paths to my destination. I assumed everyone I met was an informant. I trusted no one.

But no matter what I did, I never felt safe. I was never at peace.

I made good money. I owned nice things. I had achieved my goals, as sick and twisted as they were. I had won - but my prize was constant fear.

One afternoon, several months after my first visit to the House, I experienced a moment of awareness; it was like I startled awake only to find myself in a bad dream. I was in a dark basement, surrounded by desperate people; each in terrible pain of one kind or another. They passed a pipe, ingesting poison in order to feel better for a little while.

I watched them, and for a few minutes I knew it was all wrong. I closed my eyes and remembered: a happy childhood, sunny afternoons, Sunday morning going to mass. Kneeling and receiving the sacrament, the taste of it, the peace of the church around me. I had turned my back on all of it. I had climbed into the belly of the beast where everything was dark. When I opened my eyes I decided to go home. Talk to my mom. Get help. Then someone passed the pipe and... I was fine. I regained control. I owned the world.

Later, as I drove home, I turned down my street and almost ran into a black Durango. The driver inched forward, as if searching for an address. I tracked it in my mirrors as I pulled into my driveway. It pulled to a stop across the street. After a few moments, the driver's window rolled down and a man pointed a camera towards me; he took pictures of my garage, my truck, my house.

Some deep male instinct to protect my wife and home kicked in and the world turned red. Driving hard in reverse, I pulled back into the street, cursing out my window, and skidded up to the Durango's rear bumper. Before I could leap out, the driver peeled forward. He drove slowly and stuck the camera out his window to point back towards me. I chased him, honking and screaming, inches from his bumper. At the first intersection he came to a complete stop then turned left. I followed, staying as close as I could.

A half a block later the adrenaline eased off and it became obvious I was doing something stupid - I was probably tailing an investigator. I had glass in my car and in my house and I was screaming at a cop.

I pulled over and let the Durango turn off onto a side street. I waited until he was out of sight then slammed my hand against the dashboard several times, cursing. A guy working at Taco Bell thinks a black truck is watching him, he's probably mentally ill. But as I was moving more weight than anyone else in the area, this was no paranoia. They were on to me.

I had to force myself calm so as not to do anything stupid in the short drive home. Inside, I collected the weight I had - not a lot as I was due for a trip to the House, but enough to send me to prison - and flushed it down the toilet. I watched the tan crystals swirl down the drain. I was safe for the moment, but I felt no relief.

Moreover, no one knows when their hour will come: As fish are caught in a cruel net, or birds are taken in a snare, so people are trapped by evil time that fall unexpectedly upon them.   - Ecclesiastes 9:12

Dead Man

She sputtered a string of curses blurring into non-sense. When she stopped for breath, I said, "I'll have it tonight."

"Fuck tonight," she said. "And fuck you."

I was sick of these conversations. One of the worst parts of that life: all my customers were addicts. When they needed a hit they became exposed nerves - raw, angry, no sense of humor. They became assholes, all of them.

"There's nothing I can do about it. Not right now."

I heard her spit over the phone, then scream, "You're a dead man."

Another death threat. I ignored it like the dozen others I'd received that week.

"Check back in..." I did some math. I was driving a rusty flatbed truck with a car on the back - my newly purchased '78 Monte Carlo. I planned to sand it down, repaint and rebuild the interior. My buddy had offered garage space on the other side of the river. I needed to drop off the car, hurry back home, drive to Minneapolis, get the weight, and drive back. Then I'd divide, weigh and package. Altogether, it should take less than five hours. "Check back tonight."

"I said tonight's no good."

Of course it wasn't. Part of me wanted to scream back threats of my own, but it wasn't my style.

"I got nothing for you," I said. The truck rattled across the bridge and I had to speak up. Something popped behind me.

"You're dead. Next time I see you, you're dead."

"Okay," I said. I had no energy for her - and something was wrong. My car was moving loosely back and forth on the flatbed.

"I'll chop your balls off."

"Good to know," I said, but I was no longer listening. I hung up on her screaming, and pulled onto the shoulder at the far end of the bridge. She called again and I muted the phone. I clearly had a bigger problem.

The winch was busted. It's locking mechanism refused to engage. It was an old piece of shit but I had counted on it getting me ten miles. I released my own stream of curses. Everything worked against me. That unseen force kept tripping me up, pushing me down. I grabbed a wrench and hammered against the winch. I worked the metal, fighting with it to close.

It was a cold spring day but I quickly worked up a sweat. After forty five minutes the lock was closed. I stared down at it, wrench in hand, breathing hard, daring it to spring back open. It didn't move, but I didn't trust it. I slapped some extra cables around the Monte Carlo's tires. I slammed the door behind me. Enough. It was a cobbled together mess but it should hold for five miles.

Before putting the truck in gear, I glanced at my phones. I had two Nokia burners; they could only hold two hundred phone numbers each and one wasn't enough. While messing with the winch, I'd received three calls and a dozen text messages. All were from users, most pissed off about something. This was my life. I ignored them and pulled ahead. It was a busy road and narrow. Traffic backed up behind me.

Four times over five miles I pulled over to check the cables and chains. They held but barely. I was ninety minutes behind schedule by the time I pulled into the garage.

There, the winch's lock refused to open. I screamed out in frustration. The whole day could go to hell. Everything had gone wrong. My phone kept buzzing: more pissed off users. I was done. I was sick of all of it. I wanted to quit, clean up, get a real job and spend time working on my new car.

But I couldn't. The men in Minneapolis owned me. There were no breaks. There was no quitting. There was no getting out.

I had wanted this life. With cold hands I pounded a wrench against the lock. I had lost six year of my life - my phone buzzed in my pocket - for this.

Another half hour of work and the lock sprung open. I checked the time; it was too late to get to Minneapolis.

There was a window of about an hour when I'd show up. They did not want to see me outside of this window. Since I missed it, I'd need to head up tomorrow. The day was shot.

One more time I stared at the winch. Later I would recognize it as among the greatest gifts I have ever been given, but at the time I cursed it and my own terrible luck.

I ignored the buzzing from my phones and drove home. It was late when I finally pulled into my neighborhood. The street was dark; I was exhausted and didn't check the block for strange cars. Bleary-eyed, I pulled first into my garage then stumbled into the house. All I wanted was to shower off the roadside grit and maybe play a little Xbox before going to bed.

Our house was a split level: the master bedroom and living room were downstairs, and the shower was upstairs off the kitchen. I greeted my wife. I turned on the shower and stripped off my clothes. I ran water over my wrist to check the temperature. As I waited for it warm, a bomb exploded in the basement.

*What a wretched man I am! Who will rescue me
from this body of death?   - Romans 7:24*

Late 2008

The Lord is my shepherd; I shall not want. He makes me to lie down in green pastures; He leads me beside the still waters. He restores my soul; He leads me in the paths of righteousness for His name's sake. Yea, though I walk through the valley of the shadow of death, I will fear no evil; **For You are with me; Your rod and Your staff, they comfort me.** You prepare a table before me in the presence of my enemies; You anoint my head with oil; My cup runs over. Surely goodness and mercy shall follow me all the days of my life; And I will dwell in the house of the Lord. Forever. The Lord is my shepherd; I shall not want. He makes me to lie down in green pastures; He leads me beside the still waters. He restores my soul; He leads me in the paths of righteousness for His name's sake. Yea, though I walk through the valley of the shadow of death, I will fear no evil; For You are with me; Your rod and Your staff, they comfort me. You prepare a table before me in the presence of my enemies; You anoint my head with oil; My cup runs over. Surely

No Knock

The first hit landed like a blast from a cannon. I crouched, alarmed, ready to bolt but I didn't know where. I twisted around. Dust flaked from the ceiling. Three more hits came like a bomb cluster. I skittered buck naked out of the bathroom into the kitchen. One more explosion burst through my front door. Then men shouting, a blinding burst of light, then another - flash bangs burning a hole through the carpet into the wood.

Angry voices: "Sheriff's Department! Warrant! Warrant!" Officers dressed in black. Assault rifles, M16s. I scrambled back to the bathroom. I didn't want to get shot, but I needed my underwear.

I yanked up my boxers before a gloved hand grabbed my elbow. Another slammed against my shoulder.

"Down on your belly! Down!"

I shouted, "I'm moving," but they shoved me off my

feet. My knees slammed against the doorframe as they dragged me out into the kitchen. They dropped me face first onto my belly; my cheek scraped over the linoleum.

I spit curses until my throat went raw and I could barely breathe. I convulsed with rage, yanking my arms so the plastic ties dug into my wrists.

Boots clomped by my face and around my house. Glass shattered in a nearby room and something heavy thumped against the floor. I heard my wife crying from the basement.

I said, "It's going to be okay," but there was too much noise. I yelled, "Just do as they tell you. It's going to be fine."

"That's good advice." A man stood over me. I couldn't turn my head to see above his knees. He said, "Where's your stash, Big Guy?"

I told him to go to hell.

The man encouraged me to answer with his foot. "Where's your stash?"

The winch had broken. Because the winch had broken I couldn't drive to Minneapolis. Because I couldn't drive to Minneapolis I was out of stock.

I stopped swearing and took a breath. "Downstairs," I said. "In the coffee table." I kept a little glass there for personal use.

The man stepped away. I kicked my legs, struggling to find a comfortable spot, but I had no fat to cushion my bones from rubbing against the floor. A man ordered me to stop, then yanked me up, twisting me into a sitting position. They set my wife next to me.

A police officer pulled off his helmet and sat in one of my kitchen chairs. "Ben Schmidt," he said. "We have a warrant for a no-knock search of your home." Another officer placed a printer on my kitchen table. He connected it to a laptop and printed off a document.

I heard a drill from the basement as he started the questioning. He asked where I kept my stash. I refused to answer. He asked me who supplied it. I refused to answer. He asked why the safe was empty. I told him to go to hell.

As he talked men tromped through my kitchen carrying our stuff. Some of it made sense - guns, a bong, a scale - but much of it was personal. They emptied every drawer, ripped down every picture, tore the place apart.

"What's this?" Another officer held my wife's prayer feathers. They were sacred to her and were never supposed to touch the ground.

"Please don't," she said.

He tore off the leather binding. She cried for him to stop, but he ignored her. He pressed his thumb into the feathers, separating them and then let them fall to the floor.

My wife cried in a way I had never heard before.

I had no perspective. I could not see my own role in this, how my actions and choices had led us to that moment. All I felt was hate. Hate born from drugs and humiliation. Hate for the men in our space, handling our private items, making crass jokes.

The investigator kept asking questions but I drew inward. An hour passed, then two. I glared at him, feeling my eyes bulge. Occasionally I strained against the plastic bindings around my wrists but I had stopped cursing. I barely breathed.

Finally, the men left and the inspector stepped outside. My wife had stopped crying and there was a stretch of quiet. I closed my eyes and rested my head against the wall. I had never felt so powerless or broken. My life had been torn down, man-handled, mocked and tossed away.

I took a deep breath. I was hurt. I was done. It was over.

But with that last thought there came something besides anger. It was over. Thank God, it was over. After this, a public arrest and the cops watching me? I couldn't continue what I was doing.

An officer squeezed the flesh under my arm, forcing me to stand. I started to curse, but my heart wasn't in it. My anger had dissolved into pure relief. I had reached the end and, finally, I could stop.

Jesus replied, "Very truly I tell you, everyone who sins is a slave to sin. Now a slave has no permanent place in the family, but a son belongs to it forever. So if the Son sets you free, you will be free indeed."

- John 8:34-36

Phone Call

The guard stood in the doorway of my cell, one hand on his hip, the other on the frame. I sat on the bunk; it was nothing more than a piece of metal attached to the wall. The mattress was barely an inch thick. I had been staring at the fluorescent light above my head, which was always on. It dimmed a little at night but never turned off. There was never darkness nor quiet, two things I didn't know how much I'd miss until I lost them.

I was in jail - not for selling drugs, that trial hadn't happened yet - but for drinking and driving which violated the terms of my bail agreement. It had been about a month after the no-knock arrest and I had tried to clean myself up. I worked hard to stop doing drugs, and start putting my life back together. But I felt like hell. I cut back on the glass but then made up for it with alcohol. Then I started mixing the two together, messing myself up even more than I had been before. I walked around in a daze, and I drove around too. When I saw the police lights in my rear view mirror I could only shrug as I pulled onto the shoulder. I had lost control over my life and knew it.

Now, in jail, the guard said, "You've got a call."

"Me?" I pointed at myself. My cell mate was standing near the wall. He had been pacing in little circles, then back and forth across the concrete. He had only been with me for two days but his presence made a bad situation worse. He was in for sexual assault, and rumor was it had been against a minor. No matter what he had done, there was something off about him. He was a bigger guy, round all over, and soft in the eyes and face. His hair was thick with grease and he had a smell to him; it may have been in my head, I don't know, but the guy smelled like something toxic inside was seeping out. Even stranger, he carried deodorant in his hand. Deodorant in jail was a plastic stick with a ball on top which released a thin gel when it turned. My cell mate would walk with it, fiddling with the top so deodorant dripped on the floor and left a trail behind him.

There was no place to go to get away from him - or from anyone. A glass window in the door looked out onto the main area. We had no way to use the open toilet in the back of the cell without being observed. Some guards would be cool with us tacking a washcloth over the window with our toothbrush for a few minutes, but not all of them. Except for taking a piss I didn't use the toilet for the first six days.

"Yeah," the guard nodded at me. "You. Let's move it."

I wasn't expecting a phone call and figured it could only be bad news. The ten days for violating bail were almost up, but I still faced up to seven years of prison time for the drug charges. I stood up stiffly, searching the guard's face for clues, but he only looked bored. I followed him out into the common area, my muscles tensing. The guard pointed me to a phone against the wall. Bracing myself for the worst, I picked up the receiver and brought it to my ear. It smelled a bit like lunch meat.

"Ben?" It was my wife, and the first woman's voice I had heard in a week. It sounded warm and so normal; for a moment I couldn't talk.

"Hey, I need to tell you something." Her voice faltered a little bit. "I…"

"What's going on?" I said. I was in legal trouble, financial trouble, drug trouble - what she had to tell me could be a thousand different things, all of them bad.

"I'm sorry," she said. "This is harder than I thought."

"Just say it."

My voice must have had a harder edge than I had meant because she said, "It's not bad. It's…"

There was another long moment of dead air.

"It's… Ben?"

"Yeah."

"I'm pregnant."

"*Therefore keep watch because you do not know when the owner of the house will come back—whether in the evening, or at midnight, or when the rooster crows, or at dawn.*" - *Mark 13:35*

The Cross

My body felt better almost immediately. I started eating. I drank water. I slept more naturally. Each day was an improvement over the day before - except for in my head. There, everything felt thick, like each thought had to pass through sludge to get to the surface. Often I'd lose my way in the middle of a sentence and stare off at nothing. Then, even worse, I had to deal with six years worth of shame. I had poisoned people. I had used people. I had scared people. I had hurt people. I had been a tweaker, a dealer and a monster. The guilt crushed me, and on top of it all, I had to finally process the grief over losing my cousin and aunt.

In short, sobriety sucked.

And I couldn't handle it any more. I had been home from jail for a little over a week. Around me the house was dead quiet; my wife was home but asleep downstairs. Some light from the bathroom spilled onto the floor near my chair, but otherwise it was dark.

I rested my head on the kitchen table; I needed a hit. Not a lot, not to get messed up, but it had been two weeks and I needed a little cushion from the pain.

There was a bag of dope hidden in the cabinet behind the coffee grounds, almost in arm's reach, and a pipe in the basement. I'd have to move so as not to wake my wife, but she was a heavy sleeper. Once I had the drugs and the pipe, muscle memory would take care of the rest; I'd melt the crystals and suck in the smoke - I could almost taste the metallic flavor, the hint of gasoline - and all the bad feelings would burn away.

It was stupid, sitting there feeling like crap when relief was so close. No one would be hurt. It wasn't like I'd start selling again. A single hit to get me through one night, maybe two, and that would be it. I'd feel better. I'd have the energy to search for a job in the morning. And shoot, if I had a job, a real job, it would make me a better husband now and, when the time came, a better father.

I knew these were all lies as I thought them, but it didn't matter; I just needed the hit and had already wasted enough energy fighting it. I stood and a thrill ran through me as I reached for the baggie next to the stove. Now that relief was on its way, my body relaxed - all my muscles unclenched.

I pinched the plastic with my fingertips and peered at the tan crystals, gauging expertly how much I had. It would do. But when I started hurrying towards the basement to find the pipe, I was stopped by a violence.

A sound, a force of wind like a tornado, rumbled underneath the floor. Darkness and noise swallowed me whole. What felt like a fist squeezed my body from my hips to my neck so I couldn't move. My lungs refused air. My heart beat at my ribcage so hard it hurt. It was a waking nightmare - and then it stopped. The resulting quiet hurt my ears.

Slowly, my muscles relaxed enough so I could breathe. Having no idea what I had experienced or if it would come happen again, I moved carefully, testing the strength of my limbs. The floor felt soft but my legs took me across the kitchen. I stepped lightly so as not to stir the air around me. My first priority hadn't changed: get my pipe. If the world was coming to an end, I didn't want to face it sober.

I crept downstairs into the living room. The pipe was in the coffee table, but I froze up halfway across the floor.

I had visited a Hobby Lobby the day before. I had wandered the aisles aimlessly, no place to be. Nothing had interested me until, in a side aisle, my eyes landed on a cross. A wall-hanging, about a foot long, it had the 23rd Psalm etched on its surface. I had lifted it off the shelf and mouthed the words as I carefully read it through. *The Lord is my shepherd,* it said. *I shall not want.*

It was beautiful and I didn't want to put it down - so I bought it. I brought it home and had laid it flat on the coffee table in the living room.

Now, twenty-four hours later, I needed to get high. My pipe was in the drawer. The drawer was under the cross. And the cross was not were I had left it. Needles crept up my back. No longer flat, it had been placed upright and balanced carefully on its side; half in shadow, half bathed by the streetlights cutting through the drapes. It made no sense for my wife to have done that - and there had been no one else here.

Hoping to reset my brain, I closed my eyes and counted, but when I opened them the cross remained upright.

Like I was approaching a snarling dog, I took a terrible step forward and snatched it off the table. I gaped at it, barely breathing. *He leads me in the paths of righteousness,* I read. *For his name's sake.* The words were just this side of gibberish and I had to read them again and again, puzzling over the meaning. I could have stayed that way through dawn but the walls began to tremble. The violence, the rush of wind, rumbled again through my house.

I left the pipe and clutched the cross as I sprinted into the bedroom. I knelt on the mattress and shook my wife's shoulder.

"Did you hear that?"

She muttered in her sleep.

"That noise? Did you hear it?"

"Ben," she took a gentle swat at me. "I'm sleeping."

"But did you hear the noise?"

"Go to bed."

"But -"

"Stop it! I'm sleeping."

I retreated back into the living room and lowered myself onto the couch. We were in imminent danger.

Nothing was solid; the walls, the floor, my house, all could collapse with the next gust of wind. Sweat beaded on my forehead, dampened my hair; I could taste it on my upper lip. There was no escape.

He leads me beside the still waters, I read. *He restores my soul.*

Still waters, I thought. I traced the etching with my thumb. Still waters. Behind my mother's house was a shallow pond - more swamp than anything, but it was 'still water.' Was it a sign? A message from... someone? It didn't make any sense, but I knew I couldn't sit around waiting. I was a tightly coiled spring. I needed to move.

Minutes later I was in my truck rumbling towards the river. My plan was unformed: park at my mom's house, walk around back to the swamp and then... I didn't know. But it felt right, or at least better, to be out of the house coasting through the empty streets.

I stopped at a stop sign and didn't move right away. The truck idling underneath me, I picked up the cross from the passenger seat. I tried to read it, but the words jumbled in my mind. *The Lord is my shepherd.* I couldn't quite make sense of it, but it reminded me of mass. Of the low vibrations of the organ. Of my mother and father kneeling near me in the pew.

He leads me besides still waters. I took a breath and knew exactly where I was; I drove by several times a day. It was no coincidence that I had been thinking about mass - I had stopped outside my childhood church. Leaning forward, I peered up at the steeple.

Even though I walk through the valley of the shad-

ow of death. I thought of the hours spent squatting in basements, and rooms with cardboard blocking out the light. I thought of the stained couches and baseball caps pulled low over dark eyes. For six years I had embraced the shadows until shadows were all I knew.

I didn't want to feel like this any more. *Thou art with me,* the psalm read. I pulled into the church parking lot then rested my head against the steering wheel; a plastic ridge dug into my skin. I squeezed my eyes closed and huffed out a pathetic prayer, crying out to the Jesus I met in that church when I was a child.

"Help me," I prayed. "Please God, help me."

When I was done, I felt the same: shaky, afraid, awful. I leaned back, not sure what to do next.

Thy rod and thy staff, I read, *they comfort me.*

I was losing my mind, I knew it, but I had a friend named Rod and he was a Christian. He had taken a few dark turns himself but he made it out. It was two in the morning, but Rod, I thought, could comfort me. I had his number in my phone. After a few rings, he picked up.

"Schmidty… it's late," he said. His voice was mushy from sleep.

"Rod, I am…" I didn't want to finish the sentence. I was idling in a church parking lot receiving messages from a wall-hanging. I was a crazy person.

"Schmidty, listen." He sounded more awake. "Everything is going to be all right."

A cool tingle rose up my spine and with it came a distant memory of a dream. It was muddied by six years of dope, but clear enough: my cousin Tony driving his car through dark county roads with me in the passenger seat. He had turned and said, "Everything is going to be all right."

Rod said, "Call me in the morning, okay?"

Again, I couldn't speak.

Everything is going to be all right. I thought the words and something loosened in my chest. I prayed to God and he had delivered. It was my first experience with hope. Six years before I had sunk into the darkness. I had breathed it in and become its servant. But something was changing: a smudge of light had appeared. It was dim, like at the end of a long tunnel, but it was real.

Thy rod and thy staff will comfort me, the psalm read. I considered this line, let it tumble around my head as a cold wind pushed against my truck. I had talked to Rod and that had worked out. What about 'thy staff?' Custodians, secretaries, priests were part of the staff of a church. It clearly wasn't what the psalmist meant, but I was desperate. I peered out the window at the dark building. If a police officer stopped me I'd be heading for the psyche ward but I didn't care - it was time to take the leap. Gripping the cross, I trotted across the street towards the front doors of the Church of Saint Joseph.

It didn't surprise me at all to find it unlocked. I stepped inside and let the door click closed behind me. The silence had a depth to it I found unsettling, like if I listened too close I would tumble in. Unsure what to do next, I lifted the cross into the light of an exit sign. *I will dwell in the house of the Lord,* I read. *Forever.* It felt more like a warning than a promise.

Still, I had come this far and had nowhere else to go so I wandered from the entryway until I came across a heavy door. Behind it, a long corridor stretched back into darkness. I didn't know what I was looking for, but I wanted to go deeper into the heart of the church. The rubber of my soles squeaked against the floor, echoing back to me as I took a few careful steps.

Something moved at the far end; a smudge of shifting darkness, a blur. I froze, eyes wide, an icy lump swelling in my gut. The thing approached and became a hooded figure, dressed in black, all in shadows. It made no sound.

I folded over, one hand on a knee, the other pressed the cross into my chest. Light faded into darkness and the darkness choked me. Death was coming and I deserved it. Nothing would ever be all right.

I clenched and unclenched my hands. The edge of the cross dug into my palm - and with it a thought - and the thought a kind of a prayer:

He restores my soul.

In the shadow of the valley of death I will fear no evil. He is with me.

He restores my soul.

I breathed slowly. The muscles in my back relaxed enough so I could peer up. The figure glided along the corridor, but appeared less menacing. Then it turned sharp and disappeared into - a wall, a room - I didn't know.

I backed out of the corridor. I couldn't understand what I had just seen. It could have been a demon sent from hell to consume my soul, or a harmless shadow transformed by a panic attack into something more. I had no idea, but I knew this: The darkness still clung to me but the light had grown brighter. I had prayed twice that night, and both times I experienced the presence of God.

I wanted to experience it again. The doors to the sanctuary were propped open and I stepped into the cavernous room. The air was cool and smelled faintly of incense. A giant cross hung in the air over the altar; a warm light fell over it, but I couldn't find its source. A low mechanical sound, a furnace or fan, hummed underneath my own breathing.

I moved farther in. My thoughts were twisted, folded on top of each other. With each step, guilt pressed down on me, so heavy I gripped a nearby pew in order to stay upright. I shouldn't be there, I knew that. For six years, almost my entire adulthood, I had done almost nothing but bad things. The sum total of my life was absolute garbage. If someone, an angel or a priest, had grabbed me by the collar and tossed me to the street I would have understood. It would be only fair. And I'd slink home, find my hidden stash and let the darkness suck me back in.

But in the quiet of the sanctuary I did not experience God's anger. In fact, it felt more like a homecoming than a courtroom. I sat down in the pew and understood somehow that God saw me. God knew me, knew everything about me, including the worst things I had done. But He wouldn't toss me out. Instead, I felt welcomed, like the creator of the universe was glad to see me. I felt lighter, like weight had been taken off my shoulders. I felt loved, like the one who made me, cared about what happened to me. And I felt hope, like everything was going to be all right.

I spent a long time in that space, reconnecting with Jesus. When I finally stood on shaky legs I felt different. A little hungry and tired, but warm, like I had just finished laughing with a good friend.

Back in the entryway I found a table pushed against the wall. I had read the psalm so many times I had it memorized, and a line drifted in my mind: *You prepare a table before me in the presence of my enemies.* I wasn't sure about enemies, but that table seemed to have been prepared for me. Brochures lined the back; one read, "Returning to the Faith as an Adult." Another read, "Raising Your Child in the Church." I grabbed them both.

Before I could leave, some deep part of me wanted to give something back - not for the brochures, but for all of it. I patted my pockets, but had nothing on me. All I had was that cross. But, because of the events of the past few hours, that cross had become the most precious thing I owned. Without thinking, I took a name tag from a basket on the table and stuck it to the back of the cross. On it I wrote my name with the words, "I'll be back."

Outside, the streetlights shone through a gentle mist, and there was no sign of dawn. My truck was parked where I left it. Thirty minutes later, after flushing the drugs down the toilet, I laid in bed next to my wife. It was four in the morning. Her alarm would go off in three hours, but I didn't worry about that. For the first time in six years, I was at peace.

For the Son of Man came to seek and to save the lost.
- Luke 19:10

2009

The Lord is my shepherd; I shall not want. He makes me to lie down in green pastures; He leads me beside the still waters. **He restores my soul;** He leads me in the paths of righteousness for His name's sake. Yea, though I walk through the valley of the shadow of death, I will fear no evil; For You are with me; Your rod and Your staff, they comfort me. You prepare a table before me in the presence of my enemies; You anoint my head with oil; My cup runs over. Surely goodness and mercy shall follow me all the days of my life; And I will dwell in the house of the Lord. Forever. The Lord is my shepherd; I shall not want. He makes me to lie down in green pastures; He leads me beside the still waters. He restores my soul; He leads me in the paths of righteousness for His name's sake. Yea, though I walk through the valley of the shadow of death, I will fear no evil; For You are with me; Your rod and Your staff, they comfort me. You prepare a table before me in the presence of my enemies; You anoint my head with oil; My cup runs over. Surely

Awake

I startled awake but didn't know why. The windows glowed blue - morning light I assumed. I blinked a few times and the amnesia of sleep immediately gave way to dread.

Only six days left. I had to surrender myself to the detention center at the end of the week.

A man's voice said, "Schmidty. You awake?"

I jerked up, twisting to locate the source. My friend Jake leaned against the doorway to the bedroom.

"Good morning."

"What the hell, Jake?"

"Hey, sorry." He scratched the back of his neck. "Your wife let me in." His eyes were red and he looked ready to collapse. "It's about Alyssa."

The way he said her name woke me up. She had once been one of my closest friends, although I hadn't seen her since she slapped me almost a year before. At the memory I rubbed my cheek and asked, "What happened?"

"Car accident," he said. "A few hours ago."

His words didn't make any sense. It had been over three months since I encountered Jesus in His church, and I had remained sober. My body continued to feel better but my brain remained foggy. Even simple sentences took a long time for me to process.

"Ben," his voice broke. "She didn't make it."

"I don't…"

"She's dead." He buried his face in his hands. "Alyssa's dead."

Everything grew hazy. I said 'no' a few times and felt hot tears on my cheeks. At some point Jake had to leave. I laid in bed and wondered if there was any reason to ever get up. It wasn't right. It wasn't fair. I cried out to God in my prayers. There was something terribly wrong with the world if Alyssa could be taken from it.

I had thought countless times about contacting her, telling her I had cleaned up my life, but never did. I hadn't wanted her to know I was going to jail. After everything I had done, they only sentenced me to a little over two months. Due to a broken winch, I was getting off easy. Still, I was ashamed and never called her. And now it had become too late.

I attended her funeral later in the week. I left shattered, floating around in a fog of grief. I only had two days of freedom left, but I wasted them wallowing in regret over the six years I had lost. Six years I could have spent pursuing healthy friendships - I could have spent hanging out with Alyssa.

My brother, of course, decided to call that night. He had disappeared for a few months but was back and needed a ride. I picked him up outside one of the houses I now avoided. He didn't look good. A series of angry red welts climbed his neck and his eyes were tinted yellow. I wondered what happened to the kid who helped me build forts in the backyard and showed me tricks on his skateboard. He'd been gone, I knew, for a long time. But then, so had I.

Jesse had directed me to a house across town. I stopped in front of it, but he didn't get out of the car.

"Heard they're locking you up?" he said. His voice was raspy and low.

"Yeah."

"Shit."

I shrugged.

"How long?"

"About three months. Then six years of probation. If I violate probation then prison for a couple years."

"Shit."

Again, I shrugged.

"Hey little brother." He gave me a hungry look. "You want to come in with me? Get high one last time?"

In his head my brother probably thought he was helping - come in, smoke up, chill out; get some relief from your problems. And I certainly had problems: sobriety sucked. My brain didn't work right. I worried it never would. I missed Alyssa and I was going to jail. I had no job, no prospects, no idea what I was going to do when I got out. I was struggling to sleep at night and terrified of becoming a father. Fear and shame poisoned everything I did.

I said, "What the hell, Jess?"

"What?"

"I'm clean."

"Yeah, but one last time before…"

A few months earlier I would have been tempted, but the experience in church had changed me. Sure, I was sad and angry, and yes, my future seemed bleak - but I didn't have to face these things alone. Jesus was walking with me through the darkness.

"No," I said. "Hell no."

"All right, dude. No worries."

Without another word, he climbed out of my car and disappeared into the dark house alone.

For through the law I died to the law so that I might live for God. I have been crucified with Christ and I no longer live, but Christ lives in me.

- Galatians 2:19-20

The Window

A guard appeared in the doorway. He stood a little sideways, looking at something outside my cell. He nodded his head my direction and I knew I was going to have a roommate.

This was not good news. It had been a week and so far I'd had the cell to myself. I was in the county jail located downtown Red Wing, so most of the other inmates were low-level offenders, but some were hardcore gangsters, even murderers transitioning from prison on their last stop before release. Who knew what kind of person would walk through that door?

The guard took a half step back and my new roommate stooped a little through the doorway; the instinctive move of a big man. He nodded and gave me a familiar grin.

"Hey Schmidty."

"What the hell?" It took a moment for my brain to

catch up with my eyes. "Derek?"

I stood, my balance a little off from shock. I would have expected Derek to land in jail eventually for any number of reasons - he was a drug dealer and a thief - but I would never have imagined they'd place him in my unit, much less make him my cellmate.

He laughed at my surprise, giving me a moment to recover.

"It's good to see you, Schmidty."

"Yeah."

"You filled out a bit."

I patted my stomach. Without glass to suppress my appetite, I had gained a lot of weight.

"It's good to see you too," I said, but this was a lie. I had broken off contact with everyone from that world. I had thrown away my phones. I had avoided drug houses, which had been especially challenging. In almost any neighborhood around Red Wing I could duck into a house, pass out a few twenties and get high. But for six months I kept my distance and had stayed clean.

And now Derek, who was a huge part of the world I had been working hard to escape, would be sharing my cell. It made no sense, unless they were trying to get us to talk. An intercom hung next to each door; I assumed someone was always listening.

Whatever the reason, there was nothing I could do about it. So, faking a grin, I welcomed him to the shit.

It was rec time and the door was open. The unit consisted of two floors with about forty cells altogether. It was rarely full so there'd be thirty or so guys around at one time. Out in the common room people skittered around like an ant farm, coming and going in and out of their cells, guards escorting some to different areas of the facility.

Derek took it all in then turned back to set up his bunk. I asked after a few mutual friends. We talked about how long we expected to be there. Then Derek said, "Heard you were marked."

"Yeah?"

"Heard the crew in Minneapolis put out a $25,000 hit on you."

I had heard that too. A threat to ensure I kept quiet - it had weighed on me in the months before sentencing. I worried nonstop about the safety of my wife and unborn child.

"That's what they're saying, yeah."

He said, "That sucks." I agreed, and we left it at that.

Jail forced us into a pattern. We shut down our brains, lowered our heads and followed the routine. In the morning guards opened the doors and we went out to eat with dull sporks and rounded trays. Then they locked us in our cells as a group of Latino inmates cleaned. They would turn the television to Telemundo, the Spanish language channel, where pretty girls would cry all day on cheesy Mexican soap operas. Then the doors opened and we killed time until the next meal, the next day, the next month.

Most days after lunch I'd sit with my bible in a corner of the common area. There, a high window allowed a rectangle of sunshine to land. I'd read quietly, taking my time through the new testament. One afternoon, about a week after he got there, Derek squatted next to me.

"Schmidty, I've been thinking."

"Yeah? What about?"

He rested his head against the back of the wall. Across the room a woman was giving the weather report in Spanish.

"Lot of opportunities here," he said.

"Are there?"

"If someone's interested."

He was right. I knew every user, thief and asshole in a fifty mile radius of Red Wing. Except for those transitioning out of prison, everyone in jail was a former customer or associate. It gave me a certain respect. It wasn't exactly Goodfellas. I wasn't making dinner in a private room with fresh ingredients smuggled in by guards, but the other inmates treated me well. They'd offer me some extra ramen or a second piece of corn bread. They figured when we were both back outside I'd remember and get them a little weight for their trouble.

And if I was interested in the hustle, I wouldn't need to wait until I got out. Smuggling was big business. Other guys bragged they could get you anything - from meth to steroids. One guy had a cell phone. I already had the connections. All I'd need to do was start.

I could keep the hustle going right until my release. And then I'd be in a great position. Jail would give me credibility. The gang out of Minneapolis had put the hit on me, but if I drove up there and talked to them, looked them in the eye; it was risky, but the whole thing could turn in my direction. Shoot, if I handled it right, it could open up new markets. I could come out of jail stronger than I'd ever been. I could go from a major dealer in a small town to something bigger: a regional kingpin.

All it would cost me is my soul.

I said to Derek, "I'm sure you could find someone interested. But not me."

My rectangle of sunlight faded then disappeared. I placed a scrap of paper between Matthew 12 and 13 and closed the book. With a friendly nod - I had no hard feelings and wished Derek well - I stood up and returned to my bunk.

I didn't just believe in Jesus; I had met him. He shined his light into my darkness. At my lowest moment I had cried out in prayer and he rescued me. The drugs, the hustling, the outlaw lifestyle, these were dead ends. God didn't put me in this world to suck down glass and sell it to others. No, he had something in mind for me, for all of us. Even for guys like Derek. He made us for a purpose.

I sat on the thin mattress and turned towards the window. It was coated with a thick glaze but I knew what was on the other side: the steeple of my childhood church reaching into the sky. At night its light was blurry, but clear enough for me to see.

I knew Jesus. I had met him in that church. Facing the window, I closed my eyes and tried to tune out the noise of the men behind me. I asked the Lord, my shepherd, to be with me in the darkness, to lead me in paths of righteousness for his name's sake, and to restore my soul.

God is our refuge and strength,
an ever-present help in trouble.
Therefore we will not fear, though the earth give way
and the mountains fall into the heart of the sea,
though its waters roar and foam
and the mountains quake with their surging.
- Psalm 46:1-3

Feast

The snow crunched under my tires as I slowed to a stop. I turned off the car and headlights then didn't move for a long moment. The quiet night drifted in with a touch of cold. The dome light dimmed then went out. The darkness was familiar, a little too much so.

I had been out of jail for four months. The day of my release I had stepped out into the parking lot blinking at the sun. My wife had picked me up and offered me a pack of cigarettes. I sucked down two, barely breathing between puffs, before getting in the truck. I felt queasy as we drove home.

I had felt queasy almost every day since. My wife left me soon after my return. I couldn't blame her; I was a mess. The court-ordered treatment was helping but not much. I had no job. I had gained a ton of weight. I had no direction. I had no ideas. The only thing that kept me going - and that just barely - and the only thing that kept me sober - again just barely - was Jesus. The lonely nights stretched on forever and all I could do was hang on to the promise of God: My life had a purpose. My sins were forgiven. I was not alone.

Neither was I alone now sitting in that dark car. Behind me came a gurgle and a coo, then the beginning of a cry. My infant son didn't like sitting in the dark; it was time for us to go. I unhooked his car seat and stepped towards the house.

I didn't know it as I walked up the sidewalk, but six weeks from that night I would follow a friend up to Minneapolis and start work as a bouncer at a club. From there, I would get some gigs as a DJ and find an outlet in music. I would slog through the next couple of years. I'd wake up on time to get where I needed to be. I'd work a series of jobs I didn't particularly care for in order to pay my bills. I'd make impossibly slow progress towards my goals. And I'd spend long nights wrestling with God trying to understand what it was He wanted from me.

Eventually I'd go to school. It would take time, years, for my brain to feel normal again, but I'd work through it. Like a lot of twenty-somethings I'd struggle with what I wanted to do. I'd get a certificate in recording tech, thinking I might want a job in the music industry. Then I'd work towards a degree in criminal justice. I'd become a senator for the program and even elected to the Board of Directors for the college. I would get a degree in business and eventually a job I love at a major international manufacturer based in my hometown.

But all of that was in the future. As I gathered my son in my arms outside my mom's house, I had no idea how things would turn out. I felt stale and numb, like I had been living in a stranger's body for the past six years. Without the engine of meth pushing me forward, I felt slow and tired.

And I was nervous. It was Christmas Eve and I was at my first family gathering in years. My boy kicked my chest through his blanket as I stepped onto the front porch. My sister's laughter came muffled through the door.

I reached for the doorknob. I had a long road ahead of me, but I wouldn't face it alone; I had God on my side. I pushed open the door and light poured over me. With one arm my mom reached for her grandson. With the other, she gave me a hug.

So if anyone is in Christ, there is a new creation: everything old has passed away; see, everything has become new! - 2 Corinthians 5:17

Resources

The American Foundation for Suicide Prevention (AFSP)

This is a voluntary health organization that gives those affected by suicide a nationwide community empowered by research, education and advocacy to take action against this leading cause of death.

AFSP is dedicated to saving lives and bringing hope to those affected by suicide. AFSP creates a culture that's smart about mental health by engaging in the following core strategies:

- Funding scientific research
- Educating the public about mental health and suicide prevention
- Advocating for public policies in mental health and suicide prevention
- Supporting survivors of suicide loss and those affected by suicide in our mission

My family and I have supported the AFSP for many years and 10% of the profits of this book will be given to this organization. If you would like to donate, please visit www.afsp.org to give directly or learn more about their Out of Darkness Community Walks.

If you are in crisis, please call the National Suicide Prevention Lifeline at 1-800-273-TALK (8255) or contact the Crisis Text Line by texting TALK to 741741.

Afterward

When I met Ben roughly six years after the events of this book, he seemed in limbo. He came into the gym, didn't know anyone, but was friendly. He's a pretty big guy but had a gentleness to him. Over time we got to know each other and I got the impression something was weighing on him. You could probably write a book about his life at that time and call it Six Years Haunted.

I'd eventually learn that Ben had been in the belly of the beast. Sure, he'd been rescued, but when God whacks a person upside the head like he did for Ben there's still a long stretch where you don't know what to do. You know what's healthy. You know what will quench your thirst, but you don't know how to move through the pain. There is a lot of uneasiness and many missteps. As anyone who has gone through it can tell you, a person doesn't recover overnight.

Over those first six years of healing, Ben was making progress, but it wasn't easy. God was taking it slow, preparing him. In Exodus 33, when Moses is on the mountain he says, "All right God, I'm ready. Show me who you are."

But God replies, "I can't, Moses. If I did, I'd melt you." And eventually God only shows a sliver of himself. He takes it slow because it was all Moses could handle.

I could see that with Ben. Those first six years, God took it slow. He had Ben; Ben was listening, but God couldn't jump all the way into his life because it would be too much, too intense, too terrifying; it would melt him.

Then things started to tumble. He was introduced to people like John Turnipseed and Jesse Wise. These are men who had been involved in drugs, and who had spent time in prison. Both of them took their past - all the garbage and the hurt - and let God use it to heal others. Their friendship lit Ben up, offering a new way to see his own past as an opportunity for hope and healing - until ultimately God brought him to the point where he was able to sit down and tell his story.

When God puts people in your life while you're on the path to healing, you form a deep connection. God was healing a wound in me when I met Ben so I know him. I know what he's been through. And I know, I can feel it, that this next stage in Ben's life will be extraordinary.

In the forward I encouraged you to watch for Jesus on every page. Now at the end I want to encourage you to watch for Jesus in Ben's life. This next section of his journey could be titled <u>Six Years Gained</u> because God is up to something. Keep your eyes open and watch as

Jesus brings impossible healing into the world through
Ben.

> - Tom Blee, MD
> *Creator and Co-Director of LIFEteam,*
> *a hospital-based intervention program*
> Author of <u>How to Save a Surgeon</u>

Acknowledgements

To the Lord - Your love rescued me. As hard as we've worked on the book, it doesn't quite do justice to how grateful I am to have been pulled from the darkness into the light.

Caren - You are my rock. You make my life better every day, and I thank God for your support. Thank you for your feedback on this book and for helping set my life in the right direction. I love you.

To Dr. Blee - You set this project in motion. Thank you for your encouragement and the example you set in your walk with Jesus. Your words and actions inspire me to do more for others.

To Brian Scott - You took the time to hear my story. Then you dedicated countless hours to help me share it and in the process achieve a life-long goal. Thank you. May you and your family be blessed.

To John Turnipseed - You set an example of how our stories can be used to help others. And your work with Urban Ventures continues to inspire me. Thank you.

To Lu Taylor - You reached out to me immediately after I got in trouble. Thank you for your guidance, for believing in me, and for simply caring about how I was doing. I am also profoundly grateful to the many good people within the Prairie Island Indian Community who have supported me along the way.

To Travis Boyd - Our friendship has endured through everything in this book and beyond. I appreciate your steady presence in my life more than you know, especially during those difficult years as I worked to get my life together. (Still waiting to take your Mercedes out for a drive though.)

To Gloria Krause Barker - Thank you for your support, and your never-ending dedication to Suicide Awareness and Prevention. Your son's sense of humor and positivity made school a better, brighter place, and he is missed.

To my family - You brought me up in the presence of Christ. You taught me valuable lessons on respect and caring for others. The lessons you taught you me throughout my childhood remained deep within me and guided became the foundation for who I am today.

To Josh Thacker - Your friendship has helped shape me through my childhood into the present day. I am deeply grateful to you and your family for your steady support.

To Greg Cady, Akilah Childs, and Amy Whitcomb - Thank you. Your knowledge and friendship guided me through college.

To my children - A blessing: may you follow God and the beauty of life. May you be fruitful in what you do. Know today and forever that your Daddy will always love you.

About the Authors

Benjamin Schmidt lives in Red Wing, Minnesota with his two children. Since the events of this book, he has graduated with honors with a degree in Criminal Justice and an Individualized Studies degree in behavioral psychology. He now works in sales at an international corporation based in his small town. He and his family are actively involved in suicide awareness and prevention.

Brian Scott lives with his family in Red Wing, Minnesota where he is the director of 9 Foot Voice, a Christian publishing company. He has co-authored one previous book: How to Save a Surgeon with Dr. Tom Blee.

Made in the USA
Columbia, SC
04 December 2017